Dear Kip,

Wishing you all the
best on your 40th Birthday!
We look forward to spending many
more with you. It's of love,

Kathy and Ray Hads
February 11, 1997

Historic Golf Courses of America

Historic Golf Courses of America

PAT SEELIG

Foreword by Byron Nelson
Introduction by Arnold Palmer

TAYLOR PUBLISHING COMPANY
Dallas, Texas

Designed by **Deborah Jackson-Jones**

Published by Taylor Publishing Company
        1550 West Mockingbird Lane
        Dallas, Texas 75235

Library of Congress Cataloging-in-Publication Data

Seelig, Pat.
    Historic golf courses of America / Pat Seelig ; foreword by Byron Nelson.
      p. cm.
    ISBN 0-87833-858-6
    1. Golf courses—United States—Pictorial works. 2. Historic preservation—United States. I. Title.
    GV975.S44 1994
    796.352'06'873—dc20   94-17709
                                     CIP

Printed in the United States of America

10 9 8 7 6 5 4 3 2 1

Dedicated to the soul of my grandfather, Patrick Kelly.

ACKNOWLEDGEMENTS

Golf is the foundation of my life thanks to my grandfather, Patrick Lawrence Kelly. Because I was named after him, he paid extra attention to me when I was a child. Grandpa introduced me to golf at age eight. Unfortunately, he passed away when I was ten years old. But I kept playing golf, and when I do I always think of his heart and soul.

Writing *Historic Golf Courses of America* provided me with a special occasion when I visited Worcester Country Club in Worcester, Massachusetts. I stayed with my Aunt Ethel and Uncle Jack McGinn who live in North Oxford, a Worcester suburb. Ray Lajoie, the head professional at Worcester, invited me to play the course with Uncle Jack. That turned out to be the only time I ever played with him because he died of throat cancer on April 14, 1994. At least I had that time with him, thanks to *Historic Golf Courses of America*.

Several of my friends helped me do the research and compile the photographs for this book. Hal Gervertz, a golf writer in California, helped me by photographing Olympic Club. Jack O'Leary, a Boston golf writer, set me up to photograph Brookline: Doc Giffin, a golf writer and assistant to Arnold Palmer, gave me a tour of Latrobe Country Club, set me up with a tee time, and helped compile some photos from Palmer's archives. Byron Nelson, a great friend of mine who has always been my golf inspiration, was kind enough to provide photos from his personal collection. Being a friend of one of golf's most historic figures, and playing 21 of the book's 50 courses, helped me recognize America's most historic courses.

This book would not have been possible without the help of these friends as well as all the head golf professionals and club managers who provided me with valuable information, rare photographs, and access to their courses.

CONTENTS

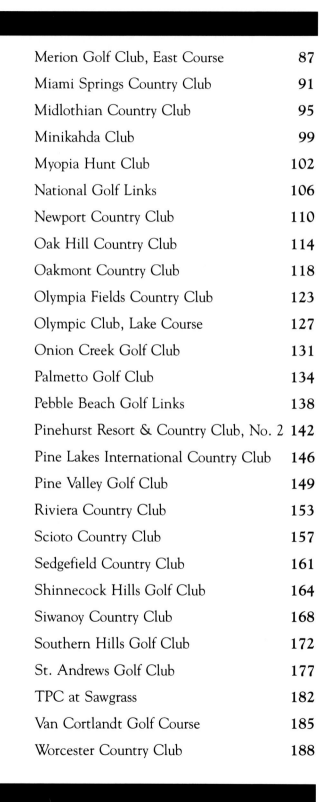

FOREWORD

The game of golf is great in itself. You can play it no matter what your age or skill level. It's also a game with a lot of wonderful history. Some of the most important and exciting matches and tournaments have been played on courses that were built even before the beginning of the 20th century. Most of these courses are still there, virtually untouched by time, bearing classic designs that are enjoyed by pros and amateurs alike.

That's why I'm glad Pat Seelig, whom I've known for many years, has done this book on America's historic golf courses. Pat ranges far and wide—from little-known Glen Garden in Fort Worth, where I got my start as a caddie and won my 18th tournament of 1945, the Fort Worth Open, to Augusta National, where I won the Masters in 1937 and 1942. He also includes in his list of fifty courses the Inverness Club, where I was pro from 1940 to 1944; Pine Valley, where Gene Littler and I played in *Shell's Wonderful World of Golf* in 1963; and Shinnecock Hills on Long Island, which has hosted the U.S. Open several times and will do so again for the USGA's centennial in 1995.

As you read, you'll find yourself wanting to visit and play many of these history-filled courses. These courses are still a joy to play, and I know Pat's dream is that they will all be preserved for future generations of golfers. I hope you'll enjoy the book and realize that these courses are among the best in the world.

Byron Nelson

INTRODUCTION

Golf is indeed the most historic sport in the world. It has been played since the 15th century and in the United States since 1888. Because I grew up on the grounds of Latrobe Country Club, golf became the foundation of my life at an early age. Its history has always been interesting to me.

I guess it is not immodest to say that I have become a part of the game's recent history, and, though I am not likely to be much more than a footnote in the 21st century, I'm certain that the game will continue to grow in popularity beyond our imaginations.

Think of what golf will be like in 2094! A decade ago I put a forecast into a century time capsule that was buried at the American Golf Hall of Fame at Foxburg, Pennsylvania. I promised not to reveal what I wrote in the letter, but I will say this: Although I expect many changes to take place in the overall picture, I anticipate that the game itself will remain much as we know it. We must take action now to insure that the traditions and history of golf are preserved for our grandchildren and their grandchildren. One step is to protect the historic course of America as they are today for future generations to experience and enjoy.

I have known golf enthusiasts who have recalled and experienced the past by playing a round of golf on a historic course with a set of hickory-shafted clubs. Who knows what will happen? Fifty or 100 years from now, steel and graphite shafts may be replaced by new technology; then it would be just as unique to play at one of our historic courses with a set of clubs that we all use today.

This focus on the historic golf courses fits into what has been a concern of mine for many years. With the game's rapid growth has come, I fear, a lessening of attention to the traditions of golf, such as its etiquette and moral codes. We should be teaching our young people that sometimes there are rules that we enforce upon ourselves. We should also be ensuring that the young pros coming into the public eye understand what the game is all about and realize that they have an obligation to preserve its traditions and its appearances. If I am to have a legacy, I would like it to be a successful effort to leave the game's traditions in the same high position that I found them as I grew up in golf.

I am pleased that Pat Seelig has chosen to include my Latrobe Country Club in his book. I think it fits the mold. Others will favor courses that failed to make Pat's list, but few will quarrel with the historical qualifications of those within the covers of this book.

Arnold Palmer

THE CASE FOR A NATIONAL REGISTER OF HISTORIC GOLF COURSES

he year is 2050. The members of Merion Golf Club, tired of their quaint but historic course, give in to a developer's request and sell the famed East Course for $500 million. The developer plans a series of luxury homesites, including a Bobby Jones Grand Slam next to the brook on the 12th hole, a Lee Trevino Rubber Snake special along the old 1st tee, a Ben Hogan Comeback overlooking the quarry, and 18 David Graham villas on all 18 greens. Somehow, the developer forgot about Olin Dutra.

The Merion members plan to use the money to build a new 8,967-yard, par-71 championship course west of the city. Robert Trent Jones IV has already been called in to propose the layout. With any luck, the 2060 U.S. Open will be held there—its first return to Merion since Eldrick "Tiger" Woods won the 2011 U.S. Open on the old 6,498-yard course with a record-shattering 263.

This scenario would make modern-day Merion members nauseated. Surely their historic East Course could never be sold to some hungry developer. This may be true in the 1990s, but today's Merion members cannot guarantee the actions of their grandchildren and great-grandchildren.

The fact that we don't know for sure establishes the case for the formation of a National Register of Historic Golf Courses. Golf in the United States has reached the point where many of the game's oldest courses have earned historic status and deserve to be preserved for future generations to admire and enjoy. Granted, many of them—particularly those constructed in the early 20th century—will probably not be competitive with courses constructed in the mid-21st century. But that isn't justification for plowing them under. Let's face it, Paul Revere's house in Boston can't hold a candle to a house constructed in the 1990s, but we still enjoy seeing it because it is a one-of-a-kind monument that is part of our nation's history. It would be unthinkable to erect a high-rise on such a site, yet, if it wasn't for the building's historic status, you could bet that a 40-story bank building would take its place.

The courses included in this book are those that need to be protected by a National Register of Historic Golf Courses. They were all chosen for at least one of five reasons—many cross over into more than one category. The first criterion was hosting a major championship. Not every course that has hosted a major is included, but those that have hosted several or one of particular historic significance have been chosen. The second selection factor was outstanding examples of a famous architect's work. Golf courses are surviving monuments to the men who shaped the way the game is played in America. Only those courses that closely resemble the architect's original design have been included.

A third reason for selection was cradles to the stars. In other words, courses where golf legends formed their games. The fourth basis of inclusion was the site of historic events. This goes beyond courses that were sites of major championship historic events to include those where other important golf moments have occurred. The final group of courses selected were the five founding courses of the USGA. Without them, golf would never have obtained its current status and widespread popularity.

A National Register of Historic Golf Courses would convey historic status on the game's most memorable courses. Historic designation would not make it illegal to destroy a historic golf course, but it just might prevent such a disaster by causing club members and course owners to treasure their courses.

Today professional women golfers compete annually in four major championships each year just as the professional men golfers do. This wasn't always the case. Women's professional golf as we know it didn't really form until after World War II, but the foundation of the modern women's golf tour began in 1937 at Augusta Country Club. A woman named Dorothy J. Mancie, known as "The General" by other women players, started a tournament at Augusta Country Club called the Titleholders. Members of Augusta National, who had just started the Masters, helped Mancie organize the Titleholders. They decided to make it the women's Masters by making the field invitation only. A player had to have won a tournament in the past twelve months to be eligible for an invitation.

"Dorothy had great interest in the game and decided to start this championship," says Eileen Stulb, past president of the Titleholders Association. "She called it the Titleholders because she wanted golfers who had earned titles to play in it." In its early years, all of the players were amateur golfers because the women's professional golf tour had not yet been established. It wasn't until 1950 that the field was mostly professional. The first winner was LPGA Hall of Famer Patty Berg, who qualified for the event by winning the Minneapolis Women's City Championship. "When I first went to Augusta, I thought, 'This is where Bobby Jones has his tournament.' It was quite an experience for such a young girl," remembers Berg. She went on to win the first three Titleholders championships and eventually four more to rank her as the only golfer to win seven individual majors in a career.

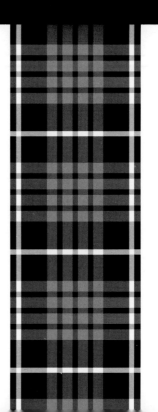

AUGUSTA COUNTRY CLUB

•

Augusta, Georgia

•

6,737 yards, par 72

•

Designed by Donald Ross

•

Redesigned by Bob Cupp

Babe Zaharias was a three-time Titleholders champion.

Marilynn Smith, a founding member of the LPGA, won the Titleholders twice.

The Titleholders rapidly evolved into the first women's major—it was founded nine years before the U.S. Women's Open. The list of Titleholders champions is indeed a who's who of women's golf; two-time winners include Kathy Whitworth, Mickey Wright, and Marilynn Smith, and Louise Suggs and Babe Zaharias each won three times.

Despite all these great women champions, the Titleholders began falling apart in the early 1960s. This was largely due to the increasing popularity of the Masters. The Titleholders Association tried to raise money but did not want a title sponsor. This made them unable to contract a commercial relationship with a sponsor the way the Masters did with Cadillac and Fireman's Fund Insurance, two companies that agreed not to tack their names on the Masters. "The Titleholders wasn't set up to make money," says Kathy Whitworth. "The Titleholders Association struggled with it for a long time, and as the LPGA Tour started to grow, the press and the players wondered why it was a major when the purses were so low." When Whitworth successfully defended her title at the 1966 Titleholders, the total purse was only $10,000 and her first place check was a mere $1,500. The Masters purse that year was $120,000, and Jack Nicklaus won $20,000 by successfully defending his title. Today a women's major championship purse is about 40 percent of a men's purse, but back then the Titleholders purse was 7½ percent of the Masters.

The Titleholders shut down after Whitworth's 1966 victory. It returned in 1972 at Pine Needles Resort in North Carolina but only for one year. Women's golf lost a major but, if it wasn't for the success of the Titleholders before World War II, the LPGA may never have been formed.

THE COURSE

The current Augusta Country Club is not exactly the same course the ladies played in the Titleholders, but its concept remains the same. Bob Cupp redesigned the 1st, 8th, and 18th holes to expand the yardage to 6,737 yards. Cupp's holes are a bit longer than the original holes, and the 18th hole saw the greatest change. It used to run down where the current driving range is and turn up to the old clubhouse that burned down in the 1960s. Now the 18th can be found where the old driving range was located and is a straight-down-the-middle, 415-yard par 4.

Augusta Country Club came along seven years before Augusta National. The 8th and 9th holes run alongside Rae's Creek, which is only about 250 yards from Amen Corner. Cupp redesigned the par-5 8th hole to be Augusta Country Club's version of Amen Corner. The original 8th had its green in front of Rae's Creek. Cupp moved it behind the creek to make it similar to the 13th hole at Augusta National. It's a straight hole instead of a sharp dogleg left. At 601 yards, it is 136 yards longer than number 13, which is located about 500 yards through the woods from the 8th green. Golfers can't easily reach the green in two like they do on 13, but, with Rae's Creek just in front of the green, 8 is Augusta Country Club's Amen Corner. The 382-yard 9th hole is just behind the 12th green at Augusta National, so Masters fans get a good view of this historic golf course while watching golfers compete for the green jacket.

Overall, Augusta Country Club is a lot like Augusta National. It has trees surrounding reasonably wide fairways that dictate a strategically placed tee shot to open up the approach

The redesigned 18th hole is different than the final Titleholders green, which is now a driving range.

to the greens. The bunkers on the course are placed so that an approach can bounce onto the green, but the pin can be placed behind the sand to set up a three putt. The Titleholders golfers played a course that is very close both physically and in design to Augusta National. Even though the Titleholders no longer exists, golfers can still enjoy the course. It's a great substitute for Augusta National, especially in the summer when the Masters course is closed.

The 9th green lies only 200 yards from the 12th green of Augusta National.

AUGUSTA NATIONAL GOLF CLUB

•

Augusta, Georgia

•

7,020 yards, par 72

•

Designed by
Alister MacKenzie
and Bobby Jones

Augusta National is by far the most celebrated golf course in America. It owes its fame to the Masters Tournament, the only major championship that is played on the same course every year. Virtually every golf fan dreams of one day playing Augusta National. In addition to its exclusivity, it's not open in the summer. So, only those lucky golfers who know a member will ever get to play the course.

Still, every great golfer since the 1930s has played there; the list of Masters champions is indeed a who's who of golf. Jack Nicklaus, Ben Hogan, Arnold Palmer, Gary Player, Byron Nelson, Nick Faldo, Raymond Floyd, Jimmy Demaret, Sam Snead, and Tom Watson are just some of the famous golfers who have won the green jacket. The Masters achieved its status as the most prestigious championship in golf largely because of the acclaim of Bobby Jones, the tournament's founder. The native of Atlanta played in the 1920s and is considered the best amateur in the history of the game. After winning the Grand Slam—the U.S. Open, British Open, U.S. Amateur, and British Amateur—in 1930, he retired from competition at the age of 28. Shortly after he retired, Jones became acquainted with Clifford Roberts, a New York-based financial consultant, and the two decided to build a national golf club in Augusta as a winter retreat for wealthy residents of the Northeast. In those days, the Carolinas and Georgia were favored winter destinations of affluent golfers. Jones and Roberts believed they could build a nationally recognized course that would lure their rich New York friends to Augusta, despite the Great Depression.

In 1931, Roberts and Jones payed $70,000

to purchase the old Fruitlands Nursery next to Augusta Country Club, a course that Jones had often played. Later, the surrounding land, which had been tied up in bankruptcy proceedings, became available. After Jones and Roberts obtained the land, they contacted Dr. Alister MacKenzie, an English golf course architect, to design the course. MacKenzie and Jones worked together to create a layout that placed a premium on strategy. It took some time to complete the course and the clubhouse, which was once the home of the Berckmans family who had owned the Fruitland Nursery. MacKenzie died shortly before the course was completed in 1933.

Jones decided to invite some of the game's

◀ *The Masters allows amateur players to spend the night in the clubhouse.*

▼ *Many Masters contenders lose the tournament by hitting their approach shot on the par-5 13th into Rae's Creek.*

best players to compete in a tournament, called the Augusta National Invitation, the next March. Roberts wanted to hold it then so that the newspaper reporters returning to New York from Florida after baseball spring training could stop off and cover the golf tournament. Because of Jones's fame and the high-caliber competition, the reporters dubbed the tournament "the Masters." Although Jones and Roberts initially resisted changing the name, they were eventually won over by popular opinion.

The Masters soon became recognized as an official major championship. At the time, only the Western Open, PGA, and U.S. Open had that status. However, because of the quality of the course and the strong invitational field, the media and golf fans began referring to the Masters as a major, and the Western Open eventually lost its major status. The Masters is unique in that it has never been played on any course other than Augusta National. This consistency means that Fred Couples, Nick Faldo, Ian Woosnam, and their peers face the same challenges as Ben Hogan, Byron Nelson, Jack Nicklaus, and Arnold Palmer did years before. Future Masters champions will have to play just as well to don the green jacket on a Sunday afternoon.

THE COURSE

MacKenzie's original design of Augusta National did not last. Jones felt that the front nine, with its many water hazards and challenging holes, posed a greater challenge and decided to flip the nines. This forced the golfers to play at their best in the homestretch to win the Masters. Five of the holes on the back nine have water hazards, and many Masters contenders have lost the tournament by hitting into the water. The 520-yard, par-5 15th hole is especially notorious. In 1985,

Ben Hogan, Byron Nelson, and Herman Keiser relax before the final round of the 1946 Masters.

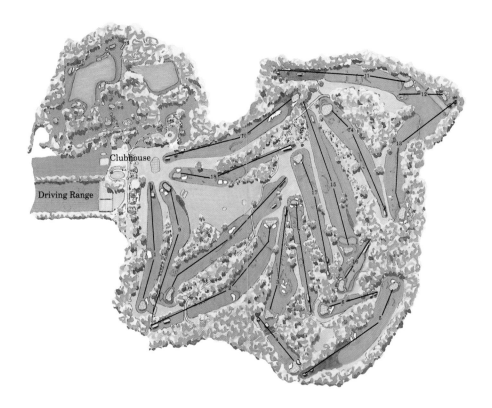

Alister MacKenzie and Bobby Jones designed Augusta National so that even the masters of the game would find it challenging.

Curtis Strange appeared headed for victory until he hit his second shot into the water on 15 and lost to Bernhard Langer. The year before, Ben Crenshaw played conservatively, laying up in front of the water on his second shot rather than risking a bath. His cautious approach resulted in a Masters win.

The heart and soul of the back nine are three back-to-back water holes at the rear of the course: legendary Amen Corner, the 445-yard, par-4 11th hole; the 155-yard, par-3 12th hole; and the 475-yard, par-5 13th hole. The pond to the left of the green on 11 forces most players to hit off to the right. Ever since the Masters instituted sudden-death playoffs in 1979, the 11th hole has been a deciding factor for many green-jacket winners and losers. Fuzzy Zoeller sunk a birdie on the 11th to win in 1979. Larry Mize's famous chip-in birdie in 1987 reinforced 11's role as a key to a Masters victory. In 1989 and 1990, Nick Faldo won playoffs on 11—the water guaranteed Faldo's victory in 1990 when

Raymond Floyd hit his second shot into the pond.

The back nine on Sunday's final round may be the crucible, but the front nine poses its own dangers. The front nine is just as long as the back nine, but the trees are their chief hazard. Holes shift from narrow fairways to wide and back again. MacKenzie and Jones believed that wide fairways demand strategy, indispensable to a good round. A tee shot at Augusta National may land in the fairway, for example, but at an angle that puts a bunker in the path of a second shot to the green.

The greens at Augusta National are known for their difficulty, and hitting the green more than 30 feet from the cup virtually guarantees a three-putt. But both nines reward good shots, and the penalties for bad ones can be overcome by great recoveries—a fitting outcome for the most intelligently designed golf course in America.

BALTUSROL GOLF CLUB, LOWER COURSE

•

Springfield, New Jersey

•

7,152 yards, par 70

•

Designed by A.W. Tillinghast

•

Redesigned by
Robert Trent Jones

Until Oakmont Country Club in Pittsburgh was host to the 1994 U.S. Open, Baltusrol Golf Club had held more Opens than any other club in the United States. Oakmont tied Baltusrol with seven, but Baltusrol remains pre-eminent, laying claim to four U.S. Open, 72-hole scoring records. No other course even comes close. In Baltusrol's first U.S. Open in 1903, Willie Anderson tied the Open record with a 307 on the original Baltusrol course and set an 18-hole record of 73. The club was quick to name Anderson head pro, a major financial benefit in the days when there wasn't a professional tour. Anderson went on to win the next two Opens, becoming the only player ever to win three consecutive Opens.

Baltusrol's only amateur U.S. Open champion was Jerry Travers, the winner in 1915. Amateurs were considered contenders more often than pros in the early 20th century because there wasn't much incentive for a golfer to turn pro back then. Pros were considered blue-collar workers, and the prize money in tournaments wasn't worth turning pro. Travers was the most unusual Open champion. With four U.S. Amateur titles, he was one of the top golfers in the country, but after he won the Open at Baltusrol he quit playing championship golf. He viewed the win as the crowning achievement of his career.

In 1936, the Open returned to Baltusrol and trumpeted a fattened purse of $5,000, a healthy sum during the Great Depression. "Lighthorse" Harry Cooper, considered the best golfer never to win a major championship, set an Open record on the Upper Course. Yet victory still eluded him. He struggled with a final-round 73 on the 36-hole Saturday, breaking the record by two strokes. The gallery hollered "Hiya champ!" when he holed out on 18. Unfortunately he had three-putted 18 and wasn't confident that he would win the Open. An unknown golfer named Tony Manero was four strokes behind Cooper after the third round. In the final round, Manero shot a front-nine 33 and cruised in with a back-nine 34. His 67 broke the record set by Cooper a few hours earlier by two shots and won him the U.S. Open in an upset with a record-setting 282.

Ed Furgol won the 1954 U.S. Open on the Lower Course with the highest score ever for a Baltusrol champion. He shot four over par, edging out Gene Littler by one stroke. No scoring records were set in the 1954 Open, but there were several firsts: The Open was televised nationally; the gallery swelled to 40,000; the prize money was $23,280; and the Open field included a record-setting 1,928 qualifying entries. Furgol was a surprise winner. A childhood accident shattered his left elbow, and he had to adapt his golf swing to accommodate the bent left arm. On the final hole, a birdieable par 5 and the easiest hole on the course, Furgol hooked his tee shot into the trees and onto the 18th hole of the Upper Course. That saved par and provided the one-shot victory.

Jack Nicklaus, the next champion at Baltusrol, smashed the record but was no surprise winner. Nicklaus won the 1967 Open on the Lower Course with a 275. Thirteen years later he won the 1980 Open on the Lower Course by breaking his own record with a 272. In 1993, Lee Janzen tied Nicklaus's record by sinking a birdie putt on 18 to defeat Payne Stewart by three strokes. This made him the second Baltusrol surprise Open champion.

Baltusrol is far less demanding than most

Jack Nicklaus won two U.S. Opens at Baltusrol, in 1967 and 1980.

other Open courses, but it has been host to so many Opens because of its location. Baltusrol is about 20 miles west of Manhattan, the former site of the USGA. In 1972, the organization moved to Far Hills, New Jersey, which is only 15 miles west of Baltusrol. When the club was only six years old, USGA officials decided to have it host the 1901 U.S. Women's Amateur, won by Genevieve Hecker. The USGA liked the course so well that Baltusrol was selected two years later for the 1903 Open.

The USGA was lucky to have Baltusrol around considering its hapless beginnings. It was opened in 1895 by Louis Keller, a New York businessman who had purchased a farm in Springfield, New Jersey, to serve as a weekend retreat. The farm had been owned in the early

The clubhouse was built in 1910 to replace the original, which was destroyed in a fire.

19th century by a man named Baltus Roll who was murdered in 1831 by two thieves. Keller decided to build a 9-hole golf course on the site of the farm. One of his friends, New York socialite Louise McAllister, came up with the name Baltusrol by putting the farmer's first and last names together and dropping the second "l." The trip to Baltusrol was an easy one for New Yorkers. As the course gained a following, Keller expanded it to 18 holes, helping attract the USGA. The club became even more popular after World War I, and the decision was made to expand to 36 holes. A.W. Tillinghast, one of the top golf architects of the era, was hired to design the new courses. The USGA liked the Tillinghast designs and held the 1926 U.S. Amateur there. Bobby Jones, who had won the two previous Amateurs, was defeated 2 and 1 by George Von Elm in the finals. That was the only defeat in the U.S. Amateur for Jones between 1924 and 1928. Baltusrol has hosted fourteen USGA national championships and will continue to remain one of the top choices of the USGA.

THE COURSE

After Robert Trent Jones redesigned the Lower Course before the 1954 Open, some Baltusrol members were displeased, especially with the 194-yard, par-3 4th hole. All the carry was over water. Trent Jones went out to the 4th tee one day with Open Chairman C.P. Burgess. Jones hit a 5-iron over the water and sank it for a hole in one. "Gentlemen, the defense rests," he said. "I think this hole is eminently fair."

Sand traps are the signature of Trent Jones's courses. The Lower Course is evidence of this, with 103 bunkers scattered over all 18 holes. Only the 4th hole is a dangerous water hole, where penalty strokes loom. But, with so many sand traps, disasters can happen at any time.

Almost all par 4s and 5s on the Lower Course have fairway bunkers and as many as six sand traps surrounding the greens. Another Trent Jones trademark is a big bunker in front of a par-3 green. The 4th hole is an exception, but the only way to reach the 9th, 12th, and

16th greens is to carry a big bunker. The same is true on approach shots on par 4s and par 5s. Most of the holes are very long, which complicates the problem. U.S. Open players play two par 5s, 1 and 7, as par 4s.

The 470-yard 7th hole tends to be the most difficult hole on the course. Trent Jones designed the green to accept a wedge shot, not the midiron that the Open players must hit. The 2nd and 8th holes are the only par 4s under 400 yards, and both are surrounded by bunkers. Players have to lay up short of fairway bunkers and then hit a midiron to the green, making the short par 4s just as tough as the longer ones.

The only par 5s in the U.S. Open are the 630-yard 17th and the 542-yard 18th. Finishing well on these holes can reverse a poor round. Birdies are quite common, particularly on 18 where golfers can hit the green in two as long as their tee shots avoid the creek that is about 325 yards out. No one in the U.S. Open reached 17 in two until John Daly gripped and ripped a driver and then a 1-iron onto the green in the second round in 1993. He made birdie, but so do other players who lay up and flop a wedge near the flag.

Of course, flopping a wedge is not always easy, nor is hitting a solid iron onto any of the greens. To make things worse, the greens on the Lower Course are firm and slick. About 65 percent of all approach shots slam onto the green and bounce well past the hole or even off the green.

Dealing with Trent Jones's classic bunkers is difficult, but the greens are even tougher. The Lower Course can be very testy for both amateurs and U.S. Open players. Only guys like Nicklaus and Janzen, when they are playing well, have consistent success at Baltusrol.

▲ *Clearing the water on the par-3 4th hole is a requirement for winning the U.S. Open.*

▼ *Robert Trent Jones's redesign of the 4th hole upset many of the members who claimed it was impossible to carry the water; Jones quieted them by stepping up to the tee with a 5-iron and acing the par 3.*

BRACKENRIDGE GOLF COURSE

•

San Antonio, Texas

•

6,185 yards, par 72

•

Designed by
A.W. Tillinghast

THE HISTORY

Mike Souchak was a burly young pro known for hammering the long ball when he ventured south to San Antonio in 1955 to play in the Texas Open at Brackenridge Golf Course, a municipal course. A.W. Tillinghast, the most famous course architect of the early century, laid out the course with casual, weekend golfers, rather than professionals, in mind. Souchak had never won in his three years on the pro circuit, but his game was well suited for Brackenridge, which had few defenses against the booming drives of the former Duke University tight end. Its wide-open spaces gave Souchak plenty of room to maneuver, and, at 6,185 yards, the par 71 seldom taxed Souchak's long or middle irons.

Souchak had a field day on the 40-year-old muni, firing rounds of 60-68-64-65. His 257 still stands as the PGA Tour record for 72 holes. "The thing I remember most was it was as cold as Willie-be-damned. One of those blue northers blew in, and I played the last round with gloves on," recalls Souchak. "The other thing is that we played off rubber mats. I guess it was because Brackenridge was a muni, and they couldn't grow grass. They had one mat to tee the ball up and another one to stand on."

Souchak got off to a phenomenal start. An 11-under-par 60—tournament par is 71—set a PGA Tour record that stood until 1977 when Al Geiberger shot a 59 at Colonial Country Club in Memphis. Souchak's score was largely due to a remarkable back-nine 27, including a wedge to the green five times and a finish on the last six holes of 3-3-3-3-3-2. Souchak describes the round as one of those once-in-a-lifetime rounds when a golfer just goes unconscious. "I didn't start so good and three putted the 5th green from 10 feet. I birdied the 6th to go one-under and then eagled the 9th to make the turn in 33," he said. "I birdied the 10th, parred 11 and 12, and eagled the 13th. From there I birdied in to shoot a 27, which was my age, for nine holes."

Souchak was on a roll. "I just couldn't wait to get to the next hole to make another birdie. I shot 68 the next day, and it felt like an 80." This was because 68 was his high round for the week. He posted the 64 just before the winds turned cold. The temperature dropped 40 degrees in one hour, and sleet and freezing rain bombarded the course as the sun took cover behind the clouds. But even Mother Nature couldn't derail Souchak's date with destiny.

Blue northers streak through Texas, bringing the temperatures down quickly. Even when the sun is shining it can be 28 degrees. Despite the cruel weather, the touring pros returned to Brackenridge for one more circuit around the course. "I had on all kinds of clothes, and I just

played well," Souchak said. "After nine holes, I had a seven-shot lead. I saw the tournament director on the green, and he told me I had it won, so go ahead and break the record." The previous PGA Tour record was 259, shot by Byron Nelson in the 1945 Seattle Open and tied in 1954 by defending Brackenridge champion Chandler Harper. Souchak matched Harper's 25-under total with two holes to go, then calmly birdied the last two holes to shoot a 65 for a 257 overall.

THE COURSE

The scorecard makes Souchak's feat look easy. After all, the yardage from the back tees is only 6,185 yards, and there are four birdie par 5s on the par 72.

But the scorecard can be deceiving. The course's slope rating is 122, making it tougher than its 67.0 rating suggests. Every tee shot and approach must be perfectly straight, espe-

Brackenridge Park boasts the largest clubhouse of any public course.

Clearing the water is the easy part of the par-3 16th hole, hitting the green is what's difficult.

cially on the front nine. Playing the front nine is like playing golf in a tunnel. Hundreds of trees line the fairways, positioned to knock slightly off-line shots either back to the golfer or deeper into the trees. The best break any golfer can hope for is the trees knocking a push, slice, pull, or hook back into the fairway. Unfortunately, that doesn't happen very often. No par 4 is over 400 yards and no par 5 over 500 yards. That sounds easy, but nearly all holes lead to double bogeys unless drives and irons are dead straight and steer clear of the trees.

For example, the toughest hole on the course is the par-4 7th hole, a modest 363 yards long. It seems unusual for a par 4 to be the toughest hole on a course, but the fairway is a scant 50 yards wide and tight with trees. When a ball goes into the trees, and it will go into the trees, all a golfer can do is chip out into the fairway and be happy with a bogey.

The fairways are a bit wider on the back nine, but the San Antonio River meanders through the second nine to make up for the difference. The 486-yard 13th hole is a classic par 5. The river runs in front of the green, so

daring golfers can go for broke, hoping to reach the green in two and putt for an eagle. The more timid golfers can lay up short of the river and loft a wedge onto the green, which sits on a rise above the river. The river cuts in front of the tee on the 497-yard, par-5 14th hole, but the carry is only about 120 yards from the back tee. The 14th is the most birdieable hole on the course because the fairway is wide and the carry is easy.

The par 3s are actually the more troublesome holes. The 200-yard, par-3 2nd hole is lined with trees and bunkers. It is easy to make four and difficult to make two. A small pond sits to the left of the 187-yard, par-3 8th hole, but only a duffed tee shot will roll into the water. On the par-3, 156-yard 16th, a large tree looms 120 yards off the tee just over the San Antonio River. Many tee shots carry the river only to hit the tree and bounce back. The 16th hole combines the best of the front and back nines, demanding a straight tee shot. Anybody who hits them will do well at Brackenridge. No one knows this better than Mike Souchak.

The green on the 18th has been redesigned since the Texas Open days, but it is still guarded by water.

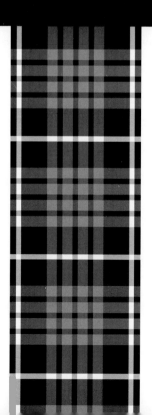

THE HISTORY

Ohio has been kind to native son Jack Nicklaus, arguably the greatest golfer of all time. The Buckeye State handed him his most celebrated victory: the 1973 PGA Championship at Canterbury Golf Club in Cleveland—the 14th major championship of his career. His win toppled the record of 13 career majors set by Bobby Jones 43 years earlier. Nicklaus now has titles to 20 majors, including two U.S. Amateurs.

Nicklaus opened at Canterbury with an even-par 72; he was five strokes behind Don Iverson and Al Geiberger and tied for 22nd. Finally, Nicklaus started playing his game. He posted back-to-back 68s to take the third-round lead. A 69 in the final round gave him a four-shot victory over Bruce Crampton. Nicklaus continued to win majors all the way up to the 1986 Masters. Walter Hagen, who won 10 career majors, is the only other double-digit major championship winner besides Nicklaus and Jones.

The two U.S. Opens at Canterbury are considered the most controversial in USGA history. Lawson Little won the 1940 U.S. Open, defeating Gene Sarazen by three strokes in an 18-hole playoff. A dispute over rules during regular play resulted in the disqualification of Ed "Porky" Oliver, who had tied Little and Sarazen with a 287. On the 36-hole final day, a storm was brewing over Lake Erie. Oliver and five other players, fearing the round would be canceled, teed off a half-hour early not realizing they were violating the rules. All six players were disqualified even though the official starter was not at the tee. Today, the U.S. Open is much more closely regulated.

However unfortunate, the disqualification did stem from a legitimate violation of the

CANTERBURY GOLF CLUB

•

Cleveland, Ohio

•

6,911 yards, par 72

•

Designed by
Herbert Strong

•

Redesigned by
Geoffrey Cornish

rules. That was not the case at the next U.S. Open at Canterbury, held in 1946, which was the first U.S. Open after World War II. The 1942 U.S. Open, scheduled at Interlachen in Minneapolis, was canceled because of the war. The USGA asked Interlachen to host the next one, but the club declined and Canterbury was selected. In the 1946 U.S. Open, the dispute was also about rules, but the decision was more controversial and the outcome more painful than in 1940.

In the third round, Byron Nelson was leading. In those days there were no permanent gallery ropes. Marshals would simply drag a rope in front of the gallery leaving players just

▶ *Lawson Little defeated Gene Sarazen by three strokes to win the 1940 U.S. Open.*

▼ *Lloyd Mangrum won the 1946 U.S. Open by defeating Byron Nelson and Vic Ghezzi in a second-round playoff.*

	HOLE	1	2	3	4	5	6	7	8	9	OUT	10	11	12	13	14	15	16	17	18	IN	TOTAL
CHAMPIONSHIP Blue Course Rating 75.8	YARDS	430	372	180	439	405	500	201	410	535	3472	360	165	372	490	385	358	605	232	438	3405	6877
MENS White Course Rating 73.9	YARDS	422	346	143	418	382	470	168	363	529	3241	352	137	348	472	369	346	590	188	391	3193	6434
	HDCP.	1	9	17	5	11	13	15	7	3		10	18	12	14	8	6	2	16	4		
	PAR	4	4	3	4	4	5	3	4	5	36	4	3	4	5	4	4	5	3	4	36	72
MATCH	WE THEY																					
LADIES Red Course Rating 74.6	PAR	5	4	3	5	4	5	3	4	5	38	4	3	4	5	4	4	5	4	4	38	76
	HDCP.	7	13	17	5	9	3	15	11	1		12	18	14	4	8	10	2	16	6		
	YARDS	405	331	118	401	375	453	142	356	515	3096	322	122	303	448	351	324	578	215	386	3049	6145

enough room to swing their clubs. On the 490-yard, par-5 13th hole, Nelson hit a solid tee shot and decided to lay up short of the downslope in front of the green. A throng of spectators gathered next to Nelson's ball. They had moved in so fast that the marshals had trouble roping off the area. Nelson's caddie tried to walk through the gallery to get to the ball, which was only about a foot away from the rope. The caddie ducked under the rope and did not see the ball; he accidentally kicked the ball as he broke through the gallery, advancing the ball one foot closer to the pin. Ike Grainger, a USGA official, told Nelson that he would discuss the matter with the rules committee to determine whether or not he should be assessed a penalty stroke. "A lot of people wanted to blame the caddie," Nelson said. "It wasn't his fault. The thing that was so bad is they had the ropes out, but they were so close to the ball he had no idea where the ball was."

While Grainger was talking to Nelson, Tommy Armour, the 1927 U.S. Open champion, was in the gallery protesting the penalty. Grainger advised Nelson to continue playing and get a ruling on the penalty before signing his scorecard. "I agreed to that, and I shouldn't have," Nelson said. "That cost me the tournament because I lost my concentration and played two-over par the rest of the way in. The way I was playing, there was no way I would shoot two-over par." Even though a penalty stroke was assessed, Nelson shot a 69 to take the third-round lead. However, the penalty still lingered in his mind. He shot a final-round 73, allowing Lloyd Mangrum and Vic Ghezzi to tie him and set up a three-man playoff. The final round had nearly led to a five-man playoff, but Ben Hogan and Herman Barron both three-putted on the final green to finish one stroke back. Nelson, Mangrum, and Ghezzi all shot 72 in the first round of the playoff. In the afternoon round, Mangrum was one shot ahead of Ghezzi and two ahead of Nelson going to the 18th hole. It started raining, and Mangrum bogeyed out of a bunker. Ghezzi missed a par putt to tie Mangrum. Nelson parred to lose by one stroke. This was the last time he ever played in a U.S. Open. As a result of this unique penalty situation, the USGA began setting up the permanent gallery ropes we see today.

▲ *Canterbury's undulating greens often force three-putts.*

▼ *It takes talent or luck to tee off on 1 and finish on 18 with the same ball.*

THE COURSE

anterbury is not especially long from the blue tees. However, 6,911 yards play very long when the wind comes off Lake Erie. The small greens and severe rough also add to the course's difficulty. Like most golf courses in the Buckeye State, Canterbury is thick with trees that make it difficult to do little more than chip back onto the fairway if a tee shot ends up in the woods. The course is a bit hilly, a creek runs through five holes, and a pond sits in front of the green on the 175-yard, par-3 3rd hole.

The creek doesn't cross the 1st hole, a 430-yard par 4. Instead, it stops just to the left of the fairway and short of the green. But the hole is long and hilly, so it is easy to pull a long-iron approach shot into the creek. That combination makes the 1st hole the toughest one on the course. Getting off to a good start on Canterbury is difficult, as is finishing well. The last three holes are just as vexing as the 1st. The 605-yard, par-5 16th hole is the longest hole on the course. It is perfectly straight, but its length makes it difficult to reach in regulation. Thanks to the wind, trees, and a creek, which is to the right of the green, the task is even tougher. The 17th hole is a 232-yard par 3 with a small green that is difficult to hit off the tee. At 438 yards, the 18th hole is a formidable par 4 with plenty of trees to block off-line shots. From start to finish, Canterbury can be tough; it definitely requires golfers to hit consistently good shots.

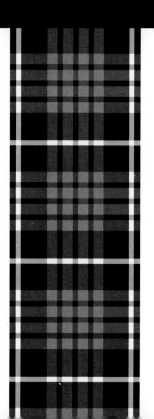

Golf got its start in the United States in the late 19th century. At the time, all major championships were played in the Northeast or upper Midwest because courses in the Southeast, West, and Southwest were considered inferior. The USGA's idea of taking golf into the South was having Columbia Country Club in Chevy Chase, Maryland, host the U.S. Open. What it finally took was money to lure a major championship to the Deep South.

Sol Dreyfuss, a Dallas banker with deep pockets, drew the PGA to his home club, Cedar Crest Country Club, by offering a $12,000 purse. This gave the 1927 PGA Championship the richest prize ever offered at that time in pro golf history. Cedar Crest became the first golf course outside the Northeast and upper Midwest to host a major championship. Besides the enticing money, another factor in the PGA's selection of Cedar Crest was the fact that it was designed in 1919 by A.W. Tillinghast, one of the most renowned golf course architects of his time. Cedar Crest is a hilly, tree-lined course out in the country several miles south of downtown Dallas. The difficulty of the course made it an excellent choice for introducing major championships to the South.

The handsome purse brought out a large field, including young Gene Sarazen, Jock Hutchinson, Long Jim Barnes, Johnny Farrell, Al Espinosa, and the Turnesa brothers. Defending champion Walter Hagen was the man to beat. He had already won four PGA Championships, including three in a row prior to the PGA. When Hagen arrived in Dallas, he announced to the field that he would win again. It wasn't an empty boast, but he didn't coast to victory. Hagen was two down with four holes

CEDAR CREST MUNICIPAL GOLF COURSE

•

Dallas, Texas

•

6,575 yards, par 71

•

Designed by
A.W. Tillinghast

to go in the 36-hole semifinal match with Espinosa. Earlier in the day, a 15-year-old caddie from Glen Garden Country Club in Fort Worth caught a ride to the tournament to watch his hero, Sir Walter, play in the semifinals. "I dogged him foot-for-foot," said the caddie, who would later join the royalty of golf as Lord Byron. "In those days they didn't have gallery ropes, so I was right beside him the whole match."

Young Byron's presence seemed fortuitous. After hitting a good drive on the par-4 13th hole (now the 407-yard 4th hole), Hagen was trying to line up his approach but the sun was making it difficult. The caddie stepped up and offered Hagen his school baseball cap to block the sun. Hagen, who shunned hats on the golf course, took the cap from the boy and wore it on his next shot. The ball landed on the green about eight feet from the hole. Hagen handed the cap back to young Byron and then sunk the putt to go 1-down. Hagen eventually tied Espinosa and won the match in one extra hole. The next day he defeated Joe Turnesa one up in the finals to win his fourth consecutive and fifth career PGA Championship. "I don't think it was that big a deal," remembers Nel-

Walter Hagen's 1927 PGA win topped off his four consecutive tournament wins that year.

son. "But my mother always loved to talk about the time I helped Hagen win the PGA."

Hagen was due to receive $2,000 in prize money. He asked Dreyfuss to pay him in the basement of the clubhouse, because there were two men upstairs waiting to attach the prize money for past-due alimony payments. Hagen took the money, shook Dreyfuss's hand, and hightailed it to Union Station to catch an early train. He got away with the money. Two years

HOLE	1	2	3	4	5	6	7	8	9	OUT	10	11	12	13	14	15	16	17	18	IN	TOT
BLUE TEES	635	341	209	395	364	205	561	326	310	3346	488	217	333	428	513	224	440	177	384	3204	6550
WHITE TEES	605	324	192	369	352	177	502	305	293	3119	466	205	303	404	488	204	422	165	364	3021	6140
											451	163	295	382	456		401	147	229	2723	
PAR	5	4	3	4	4	3	5	4	4	36	5	3	4	4	5	3	4	3	4	35	71
Best Ball																					
+/-																					
HANDICAP	1	10	15	7	8	16	2	12	13		5	18	11	6	3	14	4	17	9		
WOMEN'S PAR	6	4	4	4	4	3	5	4	4		5	3	4	5	5	3	5	3	4	37	75

later, Dreyfuss wasn't so lucky. The Great Depression wiped out his bank and drained him financially. Most of Cedar Crest's noveau riche were also left high and dry. The club closed and was purchased by the Shollkopf family in 1930. It was under a caretaker's supervision until after World War II when the city of Dallas purchased the course for public use.

THE COURSE

What affluent golfers lost, municipal players now enjoy: an excellent A.W. Tillinghast course that was host to a major championship. Few public courses can claim such distinction. Tillinghast only designed one other public course, so Cedar Crest offers a rare opportunity for municipal golfers to enjoy his style. Tillinghast's real challenges come on par 3s. Today, they are the toughest set of holes at Cedar Crest. The shortest is the 172-yard 17th hole, and the four others are all over 200 yards. The difficulty of these long holes is compounded by their small greens. Tillinghast's affinity for length is also obvious on the par 5s, which are all over 500 yards. The 1st hole is a par 5 that stretches more than 600 yards, giving golfers a strong dose of what's to come. The modern Cedar Crest has fewer bunkers than the original, but players must still navigate through many trees and hills to reach the pins. Even if golfers can't dodge Tillinghast's mine fields, they can take solace in knowing that they sank their spikes where Walter Hagen won the 1927 PGA Championship—on the course that hosted the first major championship outside the Northeast and upper Midwest.

The green on the par-4 5th hole is straight uphill beyond the trees.

Hitting the green on the par-3 17th hole is like kicking a field goal between two trees.

CHERRY HILLS COUNTRY CLUB

•

Denver, Colorado

•

7,154 yards, par 72

•

Designed by
William Flynn
and Press Maxwell

In the late 1950s and 1960s, Arnold Palmer was the most popular golfer on the PGA Tour. He won 60 career PGA Tour events and two British Opens but, surprisingly, only one U.S. Open. His U.S. Open victory came in 1960 at Cherry Hills Country Club in Denver. It was more than a major championship win; it was a classic Palmer go-for-broke comeback. This tournament also marked the end of Ben Hogan's career and the beginning of Jack Nicklaus's.

Seven strokes off the pace going into the final round, Palmer narrowed the gap hole by hole to close with a breathtaking 65. Palmer's feat established the 1960 U.S. Open as one of the best in the game's history. In 1960, U.S. Open contenders played 36 holes the final day. Palmer shot 72 in the Saturday-morning round to trail seven shots behind leader Mike Souchak. Six strokes ahead of Palmer was a 20-year-old amateur from Columbus, Ohio, named Jack Nicklaus. With 14 other golfers ahead of him, Palmer hardly looked like a contender. Bob Drum, a reporter from Pittsburgh, near Palmer's home town of Latrobe, approached Palmer while he was eating lunch between rounds and questioned his ability to post a decent finish. "If I shoot 65, I'll shoot 280, and 280s win Opens," Palmer said.

With 65 as his goal, Palmer began the final round inspired. He stepped up to the 1st tee, a downhill, 346-yard par 4. Thanks to Denver's mile-high altitude, Palmer had a good chance of making birdie by driving the 1st green. He missed the 2nd green but chipped in for birdie, then tapped in a three-footer for birdie on 3. As he continued, he birdied the 4th hole, parred the 5th, and birdied the 6th and 7th. He was 6-under after seven holes. The gallery

▸ *Arnold Palmer came from seven strokes back to defeat Jack Nicklaus and Mike Souchak in the 1960 U.S. Open.*

▾ *A plaque on the 1st tee reminds golfers that Arnold Palmer drove the green in the 1960 U.S. Open.*

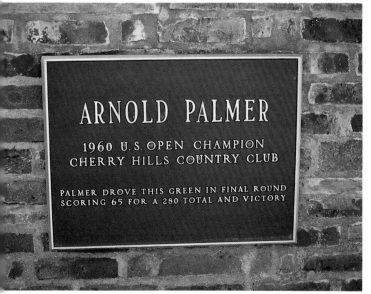

was joining the ranks of Arnie's Army. Even Drum ran out of the press room to follow Palmer. While Palmer was charging on, Souchak was collapsing. However, there were other contenders, including the 1955 U.S. Open champion Jack Fleck who shot a front-nine 32. Nicklaus was paired with Hogan. Although Nicklaus was doing well, he was slightly intimidated by the golfer he had admired as a teenager. Palmer played well coming in, with another birdie on 11 following a bogey on 10. Then he kept his promise and parred 18 for a 65 and 280.

Would 280 be good enough? Nicklaus three-putted the 13th from 10 feet, essentially ending his threat. Hogan was still in contention for a record fifth U.S. Open victory. On the par-5 17th hole, Hogan tried to loft a wedge near the pin, which was at the front of the green beside a pond. The ball splashed in and Hogan made a bogey 6. Karsten Solheim, an engineer from California, was watching from the gallery. He had just designed a set of cavity-back irons and said, "If Hogan was playing my clubs, he

wouldn't have hit it in the water." Hogan then hooked it into the water off the 18th tee for a 73. Nicklaus was calmer, posting a 71—282 to finish second, the best finish by an amateur since the 1933 U.S. Open, when John Goodman won at North Shore Golf Club.

Palmer's victory ensured Cherry Hills a place in the history of golf. But accolades were not new to the club. In 1937, the well-designed new course became the westernmost club to ever host the U.S. Open—one of the reasons for its selection was that it had plenty of parking for spectators. That year Ralph Guldahl won his second consecutive U.S. Open at Cherry Hills. In 1938, he defeated Dick Metz by six shots. Forty years later, Andy North won the first of his two career U.S. Opens at Cherry Hills. Vic Ghezzi defeated Byron Nelson 1-up in two extra holes in match play to win the 1941 PGA Championship. Hubert Green won the 1985 PGA Championship, his second career major, in a famous duel with Lee Trevino. The list of tournament winners at Cherry Hills is indeed an impressive one.

THE COURSE

During major championships, par at Cherry Hills is lowered to 71 because the 491-yard, par-5 18th becomes a 470-yard par 4. The hole is a sharp dogleg left. The fairway slopes quickly down to a lake in front of the green, which sits atop a hill. Many good golfers have hooked their tee shots, only to watch them roll down the hill and into the water. The steep hill, which demands a controlled tee shot, can determine victory or defeat. Palmer hit a 1-iron off the tee when he won the U.S. Open. During the 1960 Open, Tommy Bolt threw his driver into the lake after hooking his tee shot into the water.

◀ *The 215-yard, par 3 15th is a common site for bogeys.*
▼ *Clearing the water on the 207-yard, par-3 12th can be tricky.*

The altitude makes Cherry Hills play a little shorter than 7,154 yards. But the collection of hazards—trees, water, and deep rough—makes Cherry Hills a championship-caliber course. Before the 1978 U.S. Open, Palmer redesigned the 1st hole, the one he drove the green on in 1960, by constructing a new tee to add 55 yards to the hole. During the 1985 PGA, the players played from the drive-the-green tee. Palmer made the first seven holes look easy with six birdies. But the only possible front-nine birdie hole for most golfers is the 328-yard, par-4 3rd hole. The rest can be birdied or parred but only with superb shots.

The back nine is much tougher, even when the 18th hole is a par 5. Par is 37, and all the par 4s are more than 400 yards. Both par 3s are over 200 yards. As Hogan knows, the approach to the 17th can be tricky because of the island green that does not allow for missed shots. Other holes test patience as well. In the 1938 U.S. Open, Ray Ainsley hit a 5-iron shot to the green on the 433-yard, par-4 16th hole. The ball spun back into the creek, but it was only halfway in the water. Ainsley tried to hit the ball out of the water and duffed the shot. The ball rolled along the edge of the water back toward the tee. Ainsley kept slashing at the ball and it kept rolling back into the water. He eventually holed out for a 19, the highest score on a single hole ever recorded in the U.S. Open.

HOLE	Course Rating	Slope	1	2	3	4	5	6	7	8	9	Out
Gold	73.8	141	404	421	328	437	543	171	394	234	438	3370
Blue	72.4	136	346	415	322	425	535	165	384	226	433	3251
White	70.4	131	319	404	309	390	510	153	366	211	423	3085
Par			4	4	4	4	5	3	4	3	4	35
Handicap Strokes			15	5	13	7	1	17	11	9	3	
Handicap Strokes			13	5	7	4	1	17	9	15	3	
Par			4	5	4	4	5	3	4	3	4	36
Red	70.4/129		294	401	295	361	494	140	345	195	378	2903

10	11	12	13	14	15	16	17	18	In	Total	Course Handicap	NET	Less ESC Strokes	Posting Score
445	577	207	387	480	215	433	555	491	3790	7160				
430	533	198	381	474	181	399	545	480	3621	6872				
400	506	171	358	445	153	388	526	449	3396	6481				
4	5	3	4	4	3	4	5	5	37	72				
8	6	14	12	2	18	10	4	16						
10	4	16	14	8	18	2	12	6						
4	5	3	4	5	3	4	5	5	38	74				
369	442	116	296	413	114	376	398	421	2945	5848				

CHICAGO GOLF CLUB

•

Wheaton, Illinois

•

6,574 yards, par 70

•

Designed by
Charles Blair MacDonald

•

Redesigned by
Seth Raynor

Charles Blair MacDonald was a founder of the USGA and winner of the first U.S. Amateur. In recognition of his importance to the golf world, his home course, Chicago Golf Club in the suburb of Wheaton, was selected to host the third U.S. Open. MacDonald had designed a 9-hole course in 1892 at a site south of Wheaton. But two years later he decided to move the club up to Wheaton, where he built the first 18-hole golf course in the United States.

Later that year, MacDonald and other club members traveled to New York to meet with members from four other clubs. Together they formed the USGA. MacDonald persuaded the USGA to stage the 1897 U.S. Amateur and U.S. Open at Chicago Golf Club. He was confident that he could win the Amateur again, but he had no interest in the Open. At that time, the Open field was almost exclusively golf pros. As it turned out, MacDonald lost the U.S. Amateur on his home course. The medalist shot 174 over 36 holes but didn't make the finals. Defending champion H.J. Whigham defeated W. Rossiter Betts 8 and 6 to win again. The U.S. Open was played the following day in 36 holes of stroke play. There were 35 players, including a handful of amateurs. As it turned out, this was the last 36-hole Open.

Joe Lloyd, a 27-year-old English-born professional representing Essex County Country Club in Manchester, Massachusetts, won the tournament by one stroke over Willie Anderson, who was destined to become the greatest player of the early Opens. Lloyd's victory made history because he birdied the 450-yard, par-4 18th hole in regular play to win by one stroke. Only two other golfers have even come close to matching this feat: Hale Irwin, when he won

▲ Chicago Golf Club, built in 1894, was the first
18-hole course in the United States.

▼ Harry Vardon won the U.S. Open in 1900, the year
he toured the United States to promote Spalding's
new Vardon Flyer.

Jerome Travers won the last major staged at Chicago
Golf Club, the 1912 U.S. Amateur.

the 1990 U.S. Open at Medinah with a birdie in a sudden-death playoff, and Lee Janzen, who birdied the final hole at the 1993 Open at Baltusrol while already commanding a solid lead over Payne Stewart. Lloyd's 18th-hole birdie remains the only one in U.S. Open history to bring a win.

Lloyd needed a par on 18 to tie Anderson. Using a gutta percha ball, he blasted his drive and stroked a brassie, or 2-wood, eight feet from the hole. Lloyd holed the putt to shoot 79, post a 162, and win by one shot. The next year the U.S. Open was 72 holes. Lloyd, who finished fourth, didn't even break 80 in any one of the four rounds at Myopia Hunt Club. He later moved to France, and his accomplishment was nearly forgotten. Many golf historians would claim that no golfer ever birdied the final hole to win the U.S. Open. But Lloyd's brassie shot turned out to be one of the greatest in U.S. Open history.

Three years later, the tournament returned to Chicago, and the celebrated Englishman Harry Vardon won by two strokes over fellow countryman John Henry Taylor. Vardon was lucky to have made the cut. Because of his fame, A.G. Spalding Company developed a new golf ball in 1899 called the Vardon Flyer. Vardon toured the United States in 1900 to promote the ball, putting on exhibitions for £2,000. Vardon entered the U.S. Open, playing with his Vardon Flyer. He led by three strokes going into the 18th. On the last green, he whiffed a putt but he still won by two strokes. It was not unusual then for foreign players to win the Open, but Vardon was the first player to return to his homeland with the U.S. Open trophy. The last Open played at Chicago Golf Club was in 1911. American-born John McDermott defeated M.J. Brady and George Simpson in a playoff. McDermott shot 80, Brady 82, and Simpson 85. It was the last time any golfer would win an Open playoff finishing in the 80s.

The last major played at Chicago Golf Club before its redesign was the 1912 Amateur, won by Jerome D. Travers 7 and 6 over Charles "Chick" Evans. In 1923, Seth Raynor, MacDonald's co-architect, redesigned the course. The USGA returned to Chicago Golf Club for the 1928 Walker Cup. The United States trounced the competition 11-1, partly due to Bobby Jones's 66, which is still the course record. Fifty-one years later, the USGA held its last national championship at Chicago Golf Club. William Campbell of West Virginia, the 1964 U.S. Amateur champion, won the 1979 U.S. Senior Amateur Championship 2 and 1 over Lewis Oehmig. No national championships have returned to Chicago Golf Club since, but the club played a vital role in awakening interest in golf in the United States.

THE COURSE

MacDonald went to college in St. Andrews, Scotland, and was introduced to golf on the Old Course. Years later, its influence on his design of Chicago Golf Club was unmistakable. He constructed mounds across the fairways, sometimes by simply accentuating the contours and rises of the hilly terrain. Many greens are slightly elevated and protected by low pot bunkers. Like St. Andrews, Chicago Golf Club has very few trees, so MacDonald relied on fairway bunkers to force straight tee shots. He also designed several dogleg rights to compensate for his tendency to slice the ball. Today the course is basically the

The United States Golf Association was founded in 1894 by members of Chicago Golf Club, St. Andrews Golf Club, Newport Country Club, The Country Club of Brookline, and Shinnecock Hills Golf Club.

same. Although it isn't particularly long, the hills and bunkers make it play longer than its 6,574 yards.

The 415-yard, par-4 12th hole is a classic MacDonald hole. The hole's five fairway bunkers demand the same perfect tee shots that St. Andrews does. The second shots must reach a punch-bowl green protected by a bunker on the right. The only water holes, the 9th and 10th, are not problems unless golfers hit far off the mark. Nine is a 401-yard par 4 with a hazard about 100 yards short of the green. The water on the 133-yard, par-3 10th hole is easy to carry. Perhaps the most difficult par 3 is the 200-yard 7th hole. The green slopes away from the tee, causing long-iron and fairway-wood tee shots to land hard on the green and roll to the right toward a long bunker.

Golfers who have finessed St. Andrews can expect to post a good score at Chicago Golf Club.

COLONIAL COUNTRY CLUB

•

Fort Worth, Texas

•

7,190 yards, par 70

•

Designed by
John Bredemus
and Perry Maxwell

In February 1949, Ben Hogan nearly died in an auto accident near the west Texas town of Van Horn. The weather was foggy, and a Greyhound Bus that was passing a truck hit Hogan's Cadillac head-on. Many people, including doctors, believed that the badly injured Hogan would never play golf again. Those who knew Hogan well knew better. After two months in an El Paso hospital, Hogan returned home to Fort Worth. Even though in pain, he was already dreaming about playing golf again. By the fall, Hogan was feeling better, so he headed out to Colonial Country Club to play golf. Initially, his muscles were tight and he didn't play well. But by December, Hogan was able to complete a full round in top form. In January, he launched his comeback by nearly winning the Los Angeles Open.

One of Hogan's early sponsors was Marvin Leonard, the owner of a Fort Worth department store who founded Colonial in 1934. Because of Hogan's relationship with Leonard, he was able to take full advantage of the championship course and rebuild his game.

Colonial was the first golf course in the South to host the U.S. Open. Leonard persuaded the USGA to choose his course as the site of the 1941 U.S. Open by offering a $25,000 purse. Still, the course must have passed muster for USGA officials to have even considered a site outside the Northeast or upper Midwest.

Many of the players in the U.S. Open, however, didn't find Colonial to their liking. The weather was the spoiler. Fort Worth is quite hot in June, but that year it also rained a lot. The Trinity River, which runs beside Colonial, spilled its banks and turned the course into a quagmire. Most of the players, accustomed to

bent grass greens, were dismayed by the slow-
ness and tough grain of bermuda. One of the
unhappiest players in the first round was Craig
Wood, the 1941 Masters champion. He started
poorly, slopping through the mud and double
bogeying the 1st hole. On the difficult 466-
yard, par-4 5th hole, he hooked his tee shot
into a muddy bank. He was ready to quit in
anger when Tommy Armour, his playing partner, urged him on. "Everybody has to put up
with this stuff," he told Wood. Wood calmed
down to a first-round 73 and soon adapted to

the mud; he tied for the lead with a second-
round 71. The heat was stifling on Saturday,
the 36-hole final day. Back-to-back 70s gave
Wood a three-shot victory for his only U.S.
Open win.

After World War II, Leonard founded the
Colonial National Invitation Tournament
(NIT), which quickly became one of the most
popular and prestigious tournaments on the
emerging PGA Tour. There were two reasons
for its popularity. The first was that the field
was restricted to the best golfers. The second
was the ever-popular Hogan, who dominated
the tournament's early years. Hogan won the
first Colonial NIT in 1946, successfully defended his title in 1947, and went on to win
three more NITs. His win in 1959 was his last
career victory.

◀ *The Ben Hogan Room, filled with trophies and awards
from his career, serves as a tribute to the golfing legend.*
▼ *The stately Colonial clubhouse sets the tone for this
historic golf course.*

Hogan's ties to Colonial were enduring. In 1955, he teamed up with famous golf writer Herbert Warren Wind to write *Five Lessons: The Modern Fundamentals of Golf,* one of the most popular golf book ever written. Hogan and Wind spent several weeks at Colonial working on the book, and illustrator Anthony Ravielli joined Hogan to gain first-hand knowledge of the course.

When Hogan retired, he thanked Colonial for its unwavering support by donating all of his golf trophies and awards to the club. Today, they are displayed in the Ben Hogan Room in the clubhouse lobby, which is open to visitors. Trophies from the U.S. Open, PGA, Masters, and British Open, as well as other medals and memorabilia from Hogan's career, testify to the abiding relationship between Hogan and Colonial.

▲ *Teeing off on the par-4 17th requires a perfect shot to avoid the trees and water.*
◀ *A tight, challenging par-4, the 9th hole demands a second shot over the water.*

THE COURSE

The course at Colonial Country Club suited Hogan's game perfectly. Par is 70, making the course's 7,190 yards play extremely long. Hogan was a reasonably long hitter, and he was also very accurate. Every fairway at Colonial is tight with trees, so distance and accuracy are vital. This is especially true of the 3rd, 4th, and 5th holes, or the "Horrible Horseshoe." Originally, John Bredemus designed these three holes to be rather short and simple. The 3rd hole was a 434-yard par 4, the 4th a 148-yard par 3, and the 5th a

▲ *The 459-yard 5th hole, Colonial's signature hole, was voted by the PGA Tour pros "Hardest Par 4 on Tour."*

▶ *The 8th hole is an uphill par 3 with a three-tiered green.*

367-yard par 4. But when Leonard attracted the U.S. Open to Colonial, he hired Perry Maxwell to redesign and expand these three holes on land he had just purchased. Maxwell's new holes were extremely difficult. Three was expanded to a 470-yard par 4 with a sharp dogleg left that played even longer if the tee shot landed down the right side of the fairway. The 4th hole became a 236-yard par 3 with a highly elevated green surrounded by bunkers. Maxwell moved the 5th hole to the banks of the Trinity River and made it a 466-yard par 4 with trouble on both sides of the fairway. Modern-day players at the Southwestern Bell Colonial consider it a major accomplishment to par the "Horrible Horseshoe."

The front nine is more grueling than the back nine, but the back is far from a cake walk. Water comes into play more often on the back nine. Both par 3s, the 13th and 16th, are car-

ries over water, and a big pond sits just to the left of the 434-yard, par-4 18th hole. Water on the final hole poses ample problems for potential winners. For example, in 1984, Payne Stewart had a one-stroke lead with one hole to go. In trying to avoid the water, he pushed his tee shot over a creek on the 17th. He bogeyed, losing in a playoff to Peter Jacobsen. That's a rather common experience at Colonial. Winners prosper in the fairways and losers suffer in the trees and water.

COLONIAL COUNTRY CLUB, NORTH COURSE

•

Memphis, Tennessee

•

7,282 yards, par 72

•

Designed by
Joseph S. Finger

On June 10, 1977, Al Geiberger shot a 59 in the second round of the Danny Thomas-Memphis Classic at Colonial Country Club in Memphis. This amazing score set a PGA Tour record that was not equalled until Chip Beck shot a 59 at Sunrise Golf Club in the third round of the 1991 Las Vegas Invitational. Both 59s were remarkable, but Geiberger earned his on a tougher course. "A lot of players will come up and vouch for my 59," Geiberger said, "They say, 'You wouldn't believe the golf course he shot 59. It is one of the toughest courses on the Tour.' It makes me feel good that I was able to do it on such a hard course."

Geiberger's 59 will probably always remain the course record; the fact that the PGA Tour no longer plays there makes it even more unique. Geiberger went on to win the tournament, the tenth win of his career, because of that remarkable round. He shot 72-59-72-70 to win without a round in the 60s. Geiberger wasn't playing well going into the Colonial. "I made a slight change a week or so before," he said. "I didn't play the week before, and the week before that I putted bad. I made a putting change at home. I opened my stance because I had a tendency to aim to the right and decelerated when I got to the ball. All of a sudden I felt so free because I could swing the putter down the line." Geiberger had also adjusted his golf swing. He had been having difficulty swinging through the ball, so he lowered his hands at address, which helped him stay down and follow through.

The changes in his putting stroke and golf swing came together on June 10 to make a nearly perfect game of golf. "It was hot that day. It was over 100 degrees and totally miserable. I

▲ *The threatening water hazards at Colonial make Al Geiberger's 59 an even more impressive accomplishment.*

▶ *Colonial dedicated a shrine to Geiberger's 59, which brought the club national attention.*

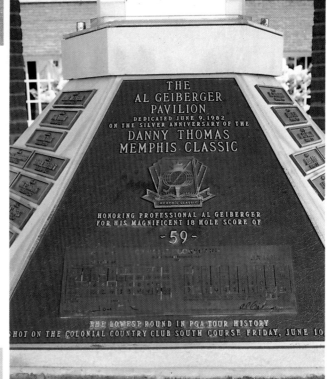

think it helped me shoot 59 because it took the attention off my score," Geiberger remembered. He started a steady round on the 10th tee. He was two under par after five holes. But the next seven holes were a tour de force: birdie, birdie, birdie, birdie, eagle, birdie, and birdie—eight under par for seven holes. On all seven, he hit the ball fairly close to the pin and made the

Players must be wary of Colonial's fast greens.

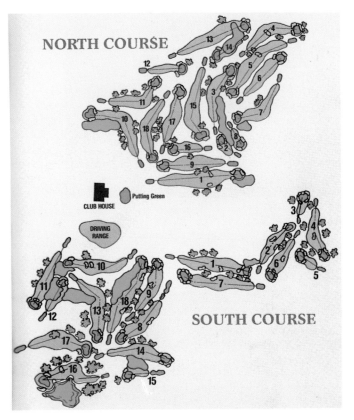

was putting for a 59, and, with the gallery yelling "59, 59," the pressure mounted. Geiberger stepped up and stroked the putt into the heart of the hole. "I raised my head up and thought, 'Thank God it's over,'" Geiberger recalled.

Colonial, no longer on the PGA tour, was also the site of two other historic events. In 1960, Ben Hogan lost a playoff to Tommy Bolt at Colonial. Had he won the playoff, Colonial would have been the golf course where Hogan won his last career tournament. The same week of Geiberger's 59, former President Gerald Ford, a golf fanatic, aced the 199-yard, par-3 5th hole—the only hole in one ever credited to a U.S. president.

THE COURSE

Geiberger's 59 was all the more astonishing because of the difficulty of Colonial. At 7,282 yards, Colonial was the second longest course on the 1977 PGA Tour. Trees, hills, fast greens, and water hazards added to the test. Eight of the holes on the back nine have water hazards, so Geiberger's start on the 10th was lucky. He was able to get the more dangerous holes out of the way early, then cruise in on the front nine. The par-5 1st hole, Geiberger's eagle hole, is a cinch for good golfers. There is a water hazard, but it's to the left and rear of the green. Several of the holes where Geiberger had his under-par binge are rather challenging. The par-5 16th hole, for example, doglegs around a water hazard, so a birdie is an accomplishment. The toughest hole on the course is the 464-yard, par-4 13th. It is a sharp dogleg right with a large pond in the corner of the dogleg. The hole invites disaster, but Geiberger parred it. Colonial will probably never see another 59.

putts with his new stroke. On the 582-yard, par-5 1st hole—Geiberger's 10th hole of the round—he holed out a 40-yard wedge shot for eagle. "The round creeped up to me. You don't start with six straight birdies because it is too hard to keep the pace going," Geiberger said. "I know because I've done that myself."

The phenomenal score attracted a large gallery. Geiberger was slightly distracted by the crowd but still confident. "The pressure built up, but the inner confidence going, because of making putts and striking the ball, made me able to handle the pressure," Geiberger said. The greatest pressure came on the 403-yard, par-4 9th hole, Geiberger's last. He hit a 9-iron eight feet from the flag. Sinking the putt would make him the first golfer to break 60 in an official PGA Tour event. Geiberger knew he

Most private golf clubs in the United States are organized as country clubs. Although their foundation is golf, country clubs include other activities, such as swimming, tennis, dining, and social events. The concept of a country club was born in 1882 at The Country Club in the Boston suburb of Brookline. Golf wasn't a part of the club at that time. A wealthy Bostonian named J. Murray Forbes wanted to form a private club where he and his wealthy friends could enjoy the New England summer weather. Forbes didn't even know golf existed at that time. His plan was to rent Clyde Park, a farm with a horse racing track, in Brookline. The club would have horse racing, a restaurant, bedrooms, a bowling alley, lawn tennis, and afternoon music. Forbes held a meeting in his Boston townhouse, and everyone agreed that forming a "country club" was a great idea. Forbes quickly signed up 404 members, each of whom paid $30 a year in dues. Most of the members were also members of Boston's Somerset Club, an exclusive men's club, and that set the standard for The Country Club membership. The concept of a country club spread quickly and soon other clubs were formed near New York, Philadelphia, and Washington, D.C.

As golf gained popularity with the likes of the Apple Tree Gang at St. Andrews, golf clubs opened all over the country. But those clubs were not country clubs. They had a golf course and clubhouse but no other recreational facilities. They were set up like British golf clubs. Once the Brookline members discovered that golf was a fine country sport, in 1892, they constructed a 6-hole golf course around the race track. Because of the Brookline members' affluence and influence, they were invited to

THE COUNTRY CLUB

•

Brookline, Massachusetts

•

7,010 yards, par 72

•

Designed by Willie Campbell

•

Redesigned by Bill Flynn and Geoffrey Cornish

meet with members from St. Andrews, Chicago Golf Club, Shinnecock Hills, and Newport Country Club to form the United States Golf Association in 1894. Initially, Brookline was not chosen to host any USGA championship because it was only a 6-hole course. However, the USGA did stage the 1902 U.S. Women's Amateur at Brookline—it was won by Genevieve Hecker 5 and 3 over Louisa A. Wells.

After the Women's Amateur, the members felt they needed an 18-hole course. So Willie Campbell designed 12 new holes in 1909, making Brookline eligible for national championships. The USGA played the 1910 U.S. Amateur at The Country Club—William C. Fownes Jr. defeated Fred Herreshoff 1-up in one extra hole. The USGA obviously approved of the new, expanded course, because it staged the

Francis Ouimet's 1913 victory made him the first amateur to win the U.S. Open.

U.S. Open there in 1913. It was right around this time that the Open replaced the U.S. Amateur as the national championship. The field of the 1913 Open was basically the same as the Opens of previous years—a handful of amateurs and a lot of foreign-born pros who had immigrated to the United States to make money through golf. The favorites were Harry Vardon and Ted Ray, two top English pros who were touring the U.S. under the sponsorship of the *London Times*. Vardon had won the 1900 U.S. Open and five British Opens; he was considered the best golfer in the world. Ray had won only the 1912 British Open. Although he wasn't as famous as Vardon, he was definitely as good.

Across the street from the Country Club lived Francis Ouimet, a former caddie of the club. Ouimet was a twenty-year-old salesman for the Boston office of Wright and Ditson, a sporting goods firm. He became a good golfer during his career as a caddie. A month before the Open, he won the Massachusetts State Amateur. As a young boy, Ouimet would cut across the golf course on his way to school. He began caddying at age 11 and would often sneak on the course to play a couple of holes. He loved golf so much that he set up his own 3-hole course on a field near his home. Ouimet only entered the Open because it was across the street from his house. He was worried that his boss would object to him taking a day off to play in the Open, because he had already taken time off to play in the U.S. Amateur and the State Amateur. Although his boss didn't mind, he never dreamed Ouimet would be in contention.

There were a record-setting 165 entries in the 1913 Open, so the USGA staged a 36-hole qualifying round. Ouimet qualified easily and

It takes a perfect approach shot to hit the 18th green and avoid deep sand traps.

shot 77 and 74 in the first two rounds. He was four shots behind the leaders, Vardon and Wilfred Reid. A third-round 74 put Francis in a tie with Vardon and Ray—Reid failed to break 80. The next day it started raining. Ray finished first with a 79 to shoot 304, which appeared to be good enough to win. Vardon putted badly on the wet greens and hardly seemed in contention. Things looked even worse after he bogeyed the 10th and 12th holes. Ouimet needed to play the final six holes two under par to shoot 79 and tie Vardon and Ray. Things were beginning to look up when he chipped in for a birdie on the 13th hole. He continued to play well by saving par after missing the green on the tough par-4 15th hole and sinking a nine-foot par putt on the 16th. On the dogleg, par-4 15th, he hit a jigger 20 feet from the hole and rolled the putt in for birdie. This tied him with Vardon and Ray. His last hole started with disaster. He missed the green and hit his chip shot

five feet short of the pin. Luckily, he sank the putt to tie the Englishmen. The gallery was thrilled to see their fellow Bostonian tied for the lead in the Open. The playoff was set for the next day.

Francis walked home and went to bed at 9:30. When he woke up the next morning it was still raining. He walked back to The Country Club where he met his ten-year-old caddie, Eddie Lowery, who was cutting school. They went to the club's polo field so Francis could hit a few balls to warm up. This was unusual because, in those days, there were no driving ranges and golfers never warmed up before playing a round. As Eddie and Francis walked back to the 1st tee, one of Francis's friends asked if he could carry his bag. Eddie was upset by the request, and Ouimet decided to stay with the caddie who had helped him tie the Englishmen. The rain only grew stronger as the playoff began. Francis drew the long straw to gain the honors on the 1st tee. He kept the honors all the way to the 5th tee. On 5, a long par 4, he followed a good drive by hitting a brassie out of bounds—back then there was no penalty stroke for going out of bounds. He hit the green with his third shot and two-putted for a bogey. Luckily, Vardon and Ray also bogeyed the hole. After five, Ray was two strokes behind Vardon and Ouimet. Vardon took the lead with a birdie on 6, and Ray birdied the 7th hole to catch up to Ouimet, who was one stroke behind Vardon. Both Ray and Ouimet birdied the 8th hole to set up a three-way tie. Pars on 9 kept them even.

As Francis was walking to the 10th tee, a Country Club member stopped him and asked how to cure his slice. After giving an informal lesson, Ouimet took the lead by two-putting the par-3 10th hole—Vardon and Ray both three-putted. A par on 12 gave Francis a two-stroke lead. Vardon birdied the 13th hole to gain a stroke. On the par-5 14th, Francis hit a solid drive but topped a brassie second shot. Lowery told him to keep his eye on the ball. Ouimet followed his advice on his third shot and hit the green in regulation. All three players posted pars, and Francis held the lead. Ray double bogeyed 15, putting him completely out of contention. Vardon and Ouimet both parred 16. Vardon took a gamble on the 17th by trying to cut the corner of the dogleg. He landed in a fairway bunker and ended up with a bogey while Ouimet parred.

Francis stepped onto the 18th tee with a three-stroke lead. Ray birdied 18 to finish with a 78, and Vardon appeared to have given up when he double bogeyed 18 to shoot 77. Francis, on the other hand, strolled in with a par for a 72 and a dramatic victory that made him the first amateur ever to win the U.S. Open.

As an amateur Open champion who defeated two top English golfers, Ouimet inspired many Americans to take up the game. There were only 350,000 golfers in the United States in 1913. Within a decade that number increased to over 2,000,000. By creating the concept of a country club, hosting an inspirational U.S. Open, and being a founding member of the USGA, The Country Club at Brookline contributed greatly to the birth of golf in the United States.

THE COURSE

The USGA returned to The Country Club 50 years later for the 1963 Open, which was won by Julius Boros in a three-man playoff with Arnold Palmer and Jacky Cupit. Twenty-five years later the 1988 Open, won by Curtis Strange in a playoff with Nick Faldo, was held there. The Country Club also hosted the 1932 and 1973 Walker Cups, both won by the United States. In 1982, Jay Sigel won the U.S. Amateur at The Country Club to become the winner of five Amateurs on the course.

The course that Boros, Strange, and Sigel won on was a bit different than the course where Ouimet won his playoff. In 1927, The Country Club added a 9-hole course called the Primrose Nine, which was intended for women, juniors, and beginners. The 18-hole course is a 6,575-yard par 71 and the Primrose Nine is a 2,999-yard par 35. When the Open is played at The Country Club, the USGA creates a 7,010-yard, par-71 course by replacing the 9th, 10th, and 12th holes of the regular course with the 1st, 8th, and 9th holes of the Primrose course. This makes the course much longer. The Country Club members frequently play a round on the "Open Course" to experience its difficulty.

No matter which holes The Country Club members play, the course is always difficult. Posting a good score at The Country Club requires accurate tee and approach shots because the narrow fairways are tight with trees and bunkers. The greens are very small and demand perfect approach shots. The toughest hole is the 445-yard, par-4 3rd, which is long and well-protected by bunkers. This hole is called "Pond" because it runs out to a pond behind the green. Although this pond doesn't come into play, one on the 411-yard, par-4 13th does. It sits off to the right of the fairway and runs up below the green. Because it is so long, golfers frequently slice a second shot into the water. During the Open, the 510-yard, par-5 11th hole plays as a 453-yard par 4 with a pond in front of the green. As a par 5, the water is easily carried with a wedge, but, as a par 4, the carry is made with a fairway wood or a wedge only after a lay-up. The Country Club's 27 holes combine to form one of the best U.S. Open courses.

▸ *Players at The Country Club take enough balls with them to replace the ones they are bound to lose in the trees.*

▾ *Trees constrict The Country Club's fairways, making straight drives a must.*

COUNTRY CLUB OF ROCHESTER

•

Rochester, New York

•

6,455 yards, par 70

•

Designed by Donald Ross

•

Redesigned by
Robert Trent Jones
and Arthur Hills

Walter Hagen was one of the best professional golfers in the U.S. in the early 20th century. Like most PGA pros at the time, Hagen discovered golf as a caddie. He was fortunate to be born in Rochester, New York, in 1892, when golf was getting its start in America. At that time, most U.S. pros were Scottish emigrants who were eager to introduce Americans to their native game. That's how Hagen discovered golf. When Hagen was only five years old, the professional at the Country Club of Rochester, a Scotsman named Sandy, put a club in his hand and encouraged him to knock golf balls around his family's living room.

Hagen was still a bit too young to take up the game. Since there weren't any junior golf programs in those days, kids were expected to learn as caddies. At age 8, Hagen started caddying at the Country Club of Rochester. He did like golf, but the real reason he started caddying was the money. He made 10 cents an hour plus a nickel tip—big money to an 8-year-old in 1900. Hagen's mother, Louise, convinced her only son to start a savings fund with the money he was making as a caddie. He made up to 95 cents a week and would dip into his savings only to buy ice cream when he wanted a treat.

Hagen's first caddie job was for a club member named Erickson Perkins. He toted Perkins's bag with its seven clubs through the front nine. On the 10th hole, there was a bunker with a tree looming on an island of grass. Perkins hit his tee shot onto the island, but Hagen didn't see it land. Their search for the ball proved futile, and Perkins fired Hagen on the spot. Refusing to give up, Hagen hung back on 10.

He rolled around in the rough, hoping he would find the ball by rolling over it. It worked. He ran back to Perkins with the ball and won his job back. At the end of the round, Hagen cleaned the clubs and pocketed a 5-cent tip. After that, he began skipping school to caddie every afternoon. On Sundays, when the club was closed, he played baseball.

Hagen eventually took up golf. One day, he saw a member, Walter Will, hitting long tee shots. Will was a much better golfer than Hagen was used to caddying for. Hagen recognized this and began copying his swing. Eventually, his own swing developed out of his imitation of Will's. There were no caddie play days at the Country Club of Rochester, so Hagen hit balls in a cow pasture. Club member John Palmer had given him a 2-iron and a 3-wood to get him started. When he was young, Hagen preferred playing baseball to golf. But, as his game improved, he spent more time on the golf course than the baseball field. Hagen was named captain of the club's caddie team, which competed against a team from nearby Oak Hill Country Club. His team won two out of three matches and was awarded trophies. That turned out to be the only amateur trophy Hagen would ever win.

Back then, caddies were declared pros by the USGA at age 16. When Hagen turned 16, Andrew Christy, the head pro at the Country Club of Rochester, hired him as an assistant pro. Finally, Hagen was allowed to play the club course. He broke 80 for the first time during a round with Christy. Inspired by Christy, Hagen continued to improve and eventually began beating his mentor in casual rounds.

Christy also helped Hagen understand the mechanicals of golf. In those days, the iron and wood heads were imported from Scotland.

Walter Hagen discovered golf at the Country Club of Rochester when he was just five years old.

Hagen assembled the clubs sold by Christy. This gave him a sense of the importance of clubs to a golfer's game. Even after he turned pro, Hagen still harbored hopes of playing professional baseball. He was pitching for the Rochester Ramblers, a semipro baseball team, and figured he would do better in baseball than golf.

In 1912, Christy and Alf Campbell, the Oak Hill head pro, invited Hagen to the Country Club of Buffalo to play a U.S. Open practice round. Hagen shot a 73, much lower than Christy and Campbell. Not wanting to be embarrassed by his assistant, Christy told Hagen to return to Rochester to take care of the pro shop. Hagen was discouraged, but Christy later allowed him to play in the Canadian Open in Toronto. He played well, scoring one stroke under 1906 U.S. Open Champion Alex Smith.

This was a turning point for Hagen. Shortly after the tournament, he took a temporary job as a pro, club manager, bartender, and greenskeeper. In the meantime, Christy decided to take a job as head pro at the Equinox Club in Vermont. Since Hagen was the former assistant pro and had experience as a head pro, the Country Club of Rochester hired him as their new head pro at the age of 19. Although he wasn't allowed in the clubhouse, he made many friends among the members who had known him as a caddie. Because of his performance in the Canadian Open, the club allowed him to play in the 1913 U.S. Open at The Country Club at Brookline. Hagen tied for fourth to finish behind Francis Ouimet, Harry Vardon, and Ted Ray. The next year he won the U.S. Open at Midlothian Golf Club in Chicago. This victory convinced him to stick with golf and give up baseball for good.

THE COURSE

A glance at the scorecard might lead golfers to mistakenly conclude that The Country Club of Rochester is an easy course. It is only 6,455 yards from the blue tees and 6,146 from the white tees. But par is 70, which means there are a lot more par 3s than par 5s. This combination makes the Rochester club a formidable challenge. The course layout also increases the difficulty. Its toughest nine is actually the middle nine, or holes 3 through 11. The front and back nine are slightly easier but only if golfers who finesse the middle nine maintain the same level of play.

The middle nine starts on the second shortest par 4 on the course. It is 332 yards but plays like it's 432. A dogleg left, it runs straight up a steep hill to the green, which rules out hitting

For many golfers, a round at the Country Club of Rochester ends with a splash.

Even though the course is only 6,146 yards, it isn't as easy as it looks on the scorecard.

a driver off the tee. A long drive will hit the bank and kick into the trees. So the tee shot must be a 4-iron short of the bank, followed by another 4-iron up the back to the green. The 212-yard, par-3 7th hole can easily lead to a double bogey. The two greatest factors are length and a creek that runs down the left side of the fairway. Even a shot that hits the green can end up in the creek.

On the middle nine, potential birdies can be blown with one poor shot. The 548-yard, par-5 10th is reachable in two by good golfers, but a push or slice will roar out of bounds. The 378-yard, par-4 18th hole is a potential birdie if a well-placed tee shot opens the approach shot away from trees and a fairway bunker. The tiny green is easy to miss, even with a pitching wedge.

The Country Club of Rochester consistently demands well-played shots. No doubt Walter Hagen honed his game after dealing with such challenges.

The trees and water hazards scattered throughout the course quickly taught Walter Hagen to be a straight hitter.

DUNES GOLF & BEACH CLUB

•

*Myrtle Beach,
South Carolina*

•

7,015 yards, par 72

•

**Designed and Redesigned
by Robert Trent Jones**

Robert Trent Jones is considered the best golf course architect of the second half of this century. His golf courses, always difficult, are outstanding because he blended the traditional designs of the early 20th century with the modern designs that emerged when steel shafts replaced hickory. His courses pose tough but realistic challenges. Trees, sand traps, and water hazards guard his fairways and greens but don't force a golfer to face unmakeable shots.

Jones was born in 1906 in Ince, England, and grew up in Rochester, New York, during the era of such golf architects as Donald Ross and A.W. Tillinghast. When Jones's parents immigrated to the United States, he was 3 years old. It was a time when Americans' interest in golf was growing quickly. Few played golf in those days. But a boy named Robert Trent Jones couldn't ignore the game at a time when Robert Tyre Jones Jr. (Bobby Jones) was the best golfer in the world. The younger Jones took up golf at a 9-hole course called Genundawah in East Rochester; he also worked as a caddie at The Country Club of Rochester. At Rochester, he caddied for Walter Hagen in a challenge match against Harry Vardon and Ted Ray.

At the age of 16, Jones played in a 36-hole tournament sponsored by the *Rochester Journal-American*. He shot 76-69—145 to finish second in the tournament and low amateur. His 69 set the course record at Genesse Valley Park Golf Course. Later, Jones dropped out of high school and found a job maintaining railroad refrigerator cars. The work didn't suit him. He remembered being fascinated by the work of Donald Ross, designer of Oak Hill Country Club in Rochester, and dreamed of becoming a golf course architect. He sought out advice, and a supervisor at his job suggested that he attend Cornell College of Engineering to learn about the profession. Jones quit his job and was hired as the golf pro, greenskeeper, and manager of Sodus Country Club, a small 9-hole club. One member, James Bashford, liked Jones a lot. When Bashford learned that Jones wanted to be a golf architect, he gave him $1,000 to finance his education at Cornell.

While there, Jones enrolled in a wide array of courses that would lay the foundation for his chosen career. He studied landscape architecture, hydraulics, agronomy, and horticulture. Although he didn't earn a degree, he mastered the basics and left Cornell in 1930 to begin his new career. With the Great Depression in full swing, however, he had trouble finding work. Finally, he was hired to design a course at Midvale Golf and Country Club in Roches-

ter. The club also hired Canadian architect Stanley Thompson to supervise. Thompson's help was invaluable to Jones. The established architect taught him to use nature as the foundation of course design and to shun greens and bunkers that clashed with the natural setting. Unfortunately, the club went bankrupt and Jones wasn't paid. That would happen to Jones three more times in the 1930s. All the while, he and Thompson worked together, and Jones continued to profit from the experience of his mentor.

With the end of World War II, Jones was on the brink of becoming the country's best golf course architect. He worked with Bobby Jones to design Peachtree Golf Club in Atlanta and later helped redesign Augusta National. Of course, his association with Bobby Jones added to his prestige. In 1947, a group of property developers in Myrtle Beach, South Carolina,

Hitting the par-3 9th green is a challenge because of sand traps and elevation.

set out to build a semiprivate club that would attract tourists to the resort city. The land they chose had been a target range for the U.S. Air Force during World War II. They hired Jones to design a top-flight course. The developers agreed that a challenging course would draw more people to Myrtle Beach. They named the club Dunes Golf & Beach Club. Although it is right on the Atlantic, the golf course was set away from the ocean.

Jones designed a superior golf course crowded with trees and South Carolina salt marshes. The Dunes Club was successful in attracting golfers to Myrtle Beach and played a major role in making the Grand Strand one of America's favorite golf vacation sites. The course was good enough for the USGA to stage the 1962 U.S. Women's Open at the Dunes. Murle Breer Lindstrom shot 301, beating Jo Anne Prentice and Ruth Jessen by two shots for her only career major. Eleven years later,

the PGA Tour conducted the final rounds of the 1973 Qualifying School at the Dunes. Ben Crenshaw won the medal by hitting the par-5 18th green in two and making an eagle.

Today, the Dunes Golf & Beach Club hosts the annual Golf Writer's Association of America Tournament the week before the Masters. The tournament was born in 1954 when Dunes Head Pro Jimmy D'Angelo invited golf writers on their way to the Masters to stop by and play the Robert Trent Jones course. D'Angelo hoped to promote Myrtle Beach as a golf resort. His idea worked well because some of the foremost golf writers, including Dan Jenkins and the late Charles Price, have won the tournament. Jenkins plays in the tournament every year and included the famous par-5 13th hole in his book, *The Best 18 Golf Holes in America*. The inclusion helped make Myrtle Beach famous and brought even more acclaim to Trent Jones.

THE COURSE

The Dunes Golf & Beach Club, designed and redesigned by the same architect, is the quintessential Robert Trent Jones golf course. By expanding the course to span more than 7,000 yards, Trent Jones acknowledged that golfers were hitting the ball much farther than when he was a kid. For example, the par 5 that Crenshaw hit in two in 1973 is now a 441-yard par 4. The water hazard in front of the green is still there, so many golfers are forced to lay up if they don't hit a good tee shot. The old par-5 tee is far off to the right and behind the new par-4 tee, which is a straight shot to the hole. Other remodeled holes include the par-4 3rd and the par-5 4th. The 3rd hole, a par

▲ *The U-turn, par-5 13th hole is considered the greatest hole of Robert Trent Jones's design career.*

▶ *The par-4 18th hole at the Dunes was originally designed as a par 5.*

5 before, is basically the same hole—it's just a little shorter. The 4th hole, originally a par 4, now has a water hazard in front of the green. The hole is only 508 yards, so golfers can go for the green in two if they hit a good tee shot over fairway bunkers at the corner of the dogleg. Otherwise, it is smart to lay up and pitch on for birdie. The par-5 15th was originally a par 4 that ran parallel to the 3rd hole.

The most famous hole at the Dunes Golf & Beach Club is the 576-yard, par-5 13th. The fairway makes a U-turn around a large lake. It is not reachable in two because a driver off the tee puts the ball too far down the fairway for a shot to the green. A long iron leads to a similar problem. The hole presents several options. Golfers may cut off as much of the water as they can by carrying across the lake with a short iron. But the lay-up leaves a long third shot, while going for broke successfully leaves a wedge to the green. The green is two levels, and three-putting is quite common when the pin and ball are on different levels. The 13th, the hole that attracted Jenkins to the Dunes, is considered the best Robert Trent Jones hole in America. Similarly, the Dunes Golf & Beach Club stands as a representation of the best golf course architect of the late 20th century.

EAST LAKE COUNTRY CLUB

•

Atlanta, Georgia

•

6,960 yards, par 72

•

Designed by Tom Bendelow

•

Redesigned by Donald Ross
and George Cobb

Bobby Jones discovered golf at the age of 5 at East Lake Country Club in Atlanta and never looked back. The East Lake course was originally part of the Atlanta Athletic Club, built in 1901. Jones's father, Colonel Robert P. Jones was a member of the Atlantic Athletic Club Board of Directors. East Lake was a popular vacation site, and, in 1907, Colonel Jones decided to rent a room in a boarding house as a summer residence. Jones was only five years old at the time, and golf was just making its way into the South.

Bobby had never heard of golf before, and he was too young to play on the course. But he did love sports, so he whiled away the hours playing baseball and tennis and fishing. One of Bobby's pals was Frank Meador, the seven-year-old son of the boarding house owner. He loved to play golf, and together he and Bobby laid out a 200-yard, 2-hole golf course in the boarding house yard. This was Bobby introduction to the game of golf.

A resident of the boarding house cut down a long iron for Bobby—this was his first club—and he used it to play on his homemade course. Golf became Bobby's passion that summer at East Lake. Just by playing on his own little course, he learned many of the rules of the game and the attitudes surrounding it.

The next summer, the Jones family moved to East Lake and purchased a house on a site that is now the club's tennis courts. His parents finally decided to take up golf, and Bobby played alongside them, toting his cut-down iron. By the end of the summer, Bobby had amassed a set of three clubs. When he was six, he played in a 6-hole junior tournament, for children ages 6 to 10, held at East Lake. 10-year-old Alexa Stern, who would grow up to win three U.S. Women's Amateurs, was the only girl playing and the best of the four golfers. She rightfully won the tournament, but the club was so embarrassed that a girl had beaten their boys that they declared Bobby the winner. Three years later, Bobby legitimately won the junior championship by scoring in the 90s.

He was already well on his way to becoming a successful golfer when Stewart Maiden, a recent emigrant from Carnoustie, Scotland, was named head pro at East Lake. Maiden became Bobby's mentor. He had an excellent golf swing, and Bobby began studying it. He would watch Maiden play and then run to the 13th hole near his home, where he would imitate Maiden's swing. By the time Bobby was 11, he shot in the 70s. At 13, he entered the Southern Amateur at East Lake. He made it to the finals of the second flight but lost 2 and 1 after shooting a 78.

Despite the loss, it was an amazing performance for a 13-year-old. The next year, 1916, Jones began playing in more presitigious tournaments. He played in most of the top tournaments in the South and won four of them, including the East Lake Club Championship. One of his 1916 wins came in the Georgia State Amateur, which was played on the Brookhaven course of the Atlanta Capital City Club. In the 36-hole final, he faced Perry Adair, another player from East Lake. Jones was a disappointing four down with 17 holes to go, but he came back to win 1-up thanks to fifteen pars and two birdies.

His victory convinced the USGA that "The Kid from Dixie" should be allowed to play in the U.S. Amateur hosted at Merion Cricket Club in Ardmore, Pennsylvania. This was the first time Jones traveled north of the Mason-Dixon Line. It was also the first time he played on bent grass greens. Although they took some getting used to, Jones mastered them quickly and shot a 74 to lead in the first qualifying round. In the first round, he defeated Eben Byers, the 1906 U.S. Amateur champion, and made it to the quarterfinals. He ultimately lost 5 and 3 to defending champion Robert Gardener, but the golf world already sensed that this 14-year-old would someday be famous.

When Bobby Jones was introduced to golf at East Lake, he took to it immediately.

Jones became the most accomplished golfer of the early 20th century. He won four U.S. Opens, five U.S. Amateurs, three British Opens, and one British Amateur. Jones quit tournament golf after winning the 1930 Grand Slam, which consisted of the British Open, British Amateur, U.S. Open, and U.S. Amateur back then. But at age 28, he had spent twenty-four years of his life playing professionally.

Blue Tees	White Tees	Par	Hcp	HOLE	Hcp	Par	Red Tees
420	405	4	3	1	5	5	402
200	151	3	17	2	15	3	146
380	354	4	11	3	13	4	323
520	480	5	15	4	1	5	465
463	441	4	1	5	7	5	436
175	158	3	13	6	17	3	140
357	342	4	9	7	9	4	322
398	375	4	5	8	11	4	356
528	512	5	7	9	3	5	458
3441	3218	36		Out		38	3048
419	404	4	2	10	4	4	363
219	171	3	16	11	18	3	142
405	361	4	14	12	14	4	345
384	355	4	8	13	12	4	345
444	426	4	4	14	8	5	409
498	486	5	10	15	2	5	440
508	490	5	18	16	6	5	459
413	382	4	6	17	10	4	349
229	202	3	12	18	16	3	161
3519	3277	36		In		37	3013
6960	6495	72		Tot		75	6061

Men's Course Rating/Slope Blue 72.9/139 White 71.6/132. Women's Course Rating/Slope 75.3/134. East Lake Country Club.

THE COURSE

George Cobb redesigned the East Lake course in 1961. His design catered to the longer shots hit by steel shafts, which replaced the hickory shafts used when Donald Ross redesigned Tom Bendelow's original layout of the course in 1915. Other than lengthening the course from 6,250 to 6,960 yards, Cobb's redesign did not differ much from Ross's. In fact, he kept many of Ross's bunkers and hole layouts and the course pattern. He did, however, enlarge the greens and bunkers and increase the number of bunkers by thirty. Cobb's redesign modernized the course. Even though today's course is not identical to the one Jones played, its challenges are as great.

Ross's bountiful use of trees, the hallmark of his design, has not been diminished by redesign. There are trees everywhere you look. The 463-

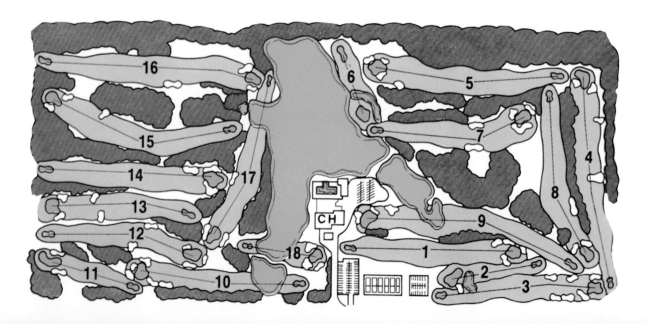

The long, uphill 18th hole is an exhausting par 3.

yard, par-4 5th hole is the course's toughest, and the trees are a major reason. The green cuts slightly to the right of a thick stand of trees, forcing a tee shot to the left toward another grove. The 498-yard, par-5 15th is only 35 yards longer but also requires maneuvering around trees only on this hole they are in the corner of a dogleg right. Frequent players of East Lake are, by necessity, masters at chipping out of the trees.

The 520-yard 4th hole, a par 5, represents a typical Ross bunker design. Bunkers to the right and left of the fairway prove to be tough traps for those who survive the trees. The only hole that traverses the lake is the 229-yard, par-3 18th, possibly the most difficult on the course to par. The carry is only about 150 yards,

The redesigned 2nd green and 3rd tee are located on the site of an old boarding house where Bobby Jones stayed as a child.

but the green sits atop a hill and is protected by two Cobb bunkers. It's tough to hit in regulation and easy to bogey. Despite East Lake's redesign, it remains a traditional golf course with fair but challenging holes.

GLEN GARDEN COUNTRY CLUB

•

Fort Worth, Texas

•

6,075 yards, par 71

•

Designed by
John Bredemus

Two of the greatest players in the history of golf came from the same caddie yard at a country club in Fort Worth, Texas: Ben Hogan and Byron Nelson. Glen Garden was an affluent club with numerous accomplished golfers among its members, but none would ever match the legacy of these two caddies. Until the 1960s, most professional golfers got their start in the game by toting golf bags. Hogan and Nelson were attracted to the job when they noticed that other boys were getting spending money by caddying, so they went to Glen Garden and applied.

The boys that were already working there did not welcome the competition for tips, so prospective caddies at Glen Garden had to survive hazing by the "Kangaroo Court" to be admitted into the caddie yard. Inductees faced various initiation rites, such as being forced to run a gauntlet of caddies who were eager to beat them and being tossed into a barrel and rolled down a hill behind the clubhouse.

Hogan and Nelson had completely opposite personalities. Hogan, who was short and slight, could be fiesty; Nelson, more reserved, was well mannered and friendly. Winning a fight with a caddie much bigger than himself established Hogan as a kid not to mess with. Nelson, on the other hand, didn't pick fights and was well liked by the members because of his polite manners.

Caddies jealously guarded their turf at Glen Garden because, in the 1920s, the USGA required them to turn professional at age 16. However, this is not the route Hogan and Nelson took. When they were both 15, in 1927, they competed in the annual Glen Garden Caddie Tournament, held the week before Christmas. It was their first of five duels during

When Byron Nelson and Ben Hogan (pictured here with Jimmy Demaret and Bobby Jones) were young caddies at Glen Garden, no one dreamed that the pair would one day play in the Masters.

their careers; Nelson would win four of them, including a playoff in the 1942 Masters. But none influenced the direction of their careers as much as the caddie tournament. When Hogan and Nelson went head to head on December 23, they knew it would be their last caddie tournament because the USGA would force them to quit caddying the next year.

None of the caddies in the tournament owned golf clubs. Members loaned players sets of hickory-shafted clubs and served as their caddies. The members considered Nelson the best player among the caddies; Hogan was regarded as just a tough kid. On the par-37 front nine, Hogan shocked the members by shooting two over par. Nelson later sunk a 30-foot putt to tie Hogan. A 9-hole playoff was necessary, and both players fought to the end. On the final hole, Nelson sunk an 18-foot putt for par to defeat Hogan by one stroke. "I got a big kick out of it because I won the tournament," remembers Nelson. "At that time, I guess Ben

didn't know me anymore than I knew him. I knew we were both caddies there, and that was it."

Nelson received a 2-iron as a prize for first place, and Hogan got a 5-iron for second. But the real reward for Nelson came later. Thanks in large part to his polite nature, Nelson was awarded an honorary junior membership at Glen Garden, which opened the door to a mul-

Byron Nelson and Ben Hogan began their lifetime love affairs with golf as caddies at the Glen Garden clubhouse.

Glen Garden is an unusually short course because it was designed for golfers using hickory shafts.

The Glen Garden course winds around a large lake.

titude of golf opportunities. He could practice and play at Glen Garden, enjoy the privileges of club membership, and play in various amateur tournaments. Hogan wasn't as fortunate. He sought a junior membership but was rejected. Forced to turn pro early, he worked in the pro shop, where he polished irons and shaved hickory shafts as Ted Longworth's assistant pro.

Meanwhile, Nelson won several amateur tournaments and waited until he was 20 to turn pro. Tournament competition gave Nelson an early advantage, and he dominated the sport in the late 1930s through the mid-1940s. When Hogan was finally able to participate in tournaments, his game was well developed, and he quickly became one of the top professional golfers of the late 1940s and early 1950s.

THE COURSE

Glen Garden hasn't changed much from the days of Hogan and Nelson's youth. Unlike many other courses, this classic early 20th century golf course was never lengthened to accomodate steel shafts. It remains its original 6,075 yards, which presents its own challenge. The course was originally nine holes. The second nine was constructed by John Bredemus in 1915. The structure of the course is always a surprise for first-time players. The par-34 back nine has an unusual format: two par 4s, then two par 5s, followed by two par 3s, one par 4, and two more par 3s. The four par 3s make the back nine play longer than its 2,926 yards. This is especially true of the downhill 237-yard 14th and the uphill 182-yard 15th. A round of golf at Glen Garden is truly unique, allowing golfers to experience an authentic early 20th century course.

Charles Blair MacDonald, who did much to promote golf in the United States, is considered the nation's first golf-course architect. He was born in Ontario, Canada, in 1856. His father was a Scottish emigrant, his mother a native Canadian. After the Civil War, his family moved to Chicago where he spent his childhood. Because of his Scottish roots, MacDonald decided to attend the University of St. Andrews. That was where he met Tom Morris, who introduced him to golf—the game wasn't played in the U.S. at that time. When MacDonald returned to Chicago in 1875, he longed to play golf. At first, he improvised at an old Civil War training camp. He would take his clubs to the makeshift course and hit balls.

In 1888, a group known as the Apple Tree Gang began playing golf. They were a highly visible group who quickly increased the popularity of golf. As the number of golfers grew, so did the need for golf courses. When a wealthy group of men in Chicago wanted a course designed, they immediately thought of MacDonald, because he was the best golfer in the country. MacDonald laid out a 9-hole course in Belmont, not too far from Chicago, and added another nine the next year. In 1894, the club moved to the Chicago suburb of Wheaton and changed its name to the Chicago Golf Club. The 18-hole course MacDonald designed for the club was the first in the United States. And so, the first golf-course architect's career was born.

MacDonald frequently played in tournaments in the Northeast. When Newport Country Club in Rhode Island decided to stage a national championship in October 1894, it invited all the best amateurs to join the field. Of

THE GREENBRIER, THE OLD WHITE COURSE

•

White Sulphur Springs, West Virginia

•

6,640 yards, par 70

•

**Designed by
Charles Blair MacDonald
and Seth Raynor**

Greenbrier was built in 1913, in part to replace Oakhurst Links that closed down in 1900.

course, MacDonald was one of those golfers. He took the first-round lead of the 36-hole event with an 89. In the second round, however, he skied to a 100 after his ball lodged against a stone wall, a popular hazard in those days. He lost the round by one stroke to Newport member W.G. Lawrence.

MacDonald was furious about losing the tournament because of the stone wall. His anger was later compounded in a tournament at the St. Andrews Golf Club, located in Hastings-on-Hudson. It was a match-play tournament, and he lost the final-round match to Laurence Stoddard, an English emigrant. MacDonald was incensed by the inconsistencies of the tournament rules. His complaints resulted in the formation of the USGA in 1894.

In 1895, the national amateur championship tournament returned to Newport, this time under the direction of the USGA. MacDonald won the match-play tournament in a 36-hole final 12 and 11 over Charles E. Sands. This win made him the first U.S. Amateur

champion and captured the attention of private club developers, who began recruiting MacDonald to design their golf courses. In 1900, he and his wife, Frances, moved to New York, where he became a partner in the stockbrokerage firm C.D. Barney & Co. As a wealthy stockbroker, he never charged a fee for designing a course. In 1902, he coined the phrase "golf architect" and persuaded other golfers, including Seth Raynor, Charles Banks, and Ralph Barton, to try this new profession. MacDonald taught all three the fundamentals of golf-course architecture, which he developed by studying numerous courses in both Scotland and the United States.

A basic tenet of his philosophy was that no course qualified as first rate unless it had 18 holes. "A first-class course must have the proper distance between the holes, the shrewd placing of bunkers and other hazards, the perfect putting greens, all must be evolved by a process of growth and it requires study and patience," MacDonald wrote in his book, *Scot-*

land's Gift: Golf. When designing a course, he looked for the right soil type and the perfect combination of undulations and hills. Important elements of his putting greens include turf quality, contour, placement, and variety. He incorporated bunkers and other hazards with meticulous attention to location and size. Finally, he insisted on variety in length, which was consistent with the needs of each hole.

All of his golf courses—half art, half science—were based on these principles. In 1913, MacDonald was invited to The Greenbrier Resort in White Sulphur Springs, West Virginia, to design an 18-hole course. The Greenbrier lay nestled in the mountains amid natural sulphur water spas. It is only a few miles from the field that was once Oakhurst Links, the first golf club in the U.S. By the time Oakhurst closed in 1900, golf's popularity had increased widely. The Greenbrier manager decided to add a course to the resort, because his guests were in the affluent class that was taking up the game.

MacDonald teamed up with Raynor to design The Greenbrier course. They tore down old brickyards and a defunct slaughterhouse

Greenbrier was one of the first golf resorts in the country.

and combined these lots with a cow pasture, sans cows, to stake out the land for the course. The Greenbrier named the course Number One, later adding two more courses. Today it is called The Old White Course. One of the first golfers to experience the course was President Woodrow Wilson on April 14, 1914, and many esteemed players have enjoyed it since. When MacDonald and Raynor designed The Greenbrier course, they created the first golf resort in America.

Landing in the beach on the par-3 15th beats splashing into the water.

THE COURSE

The Old White Course has hardly changed since its creation in 1913. It sits just below Greenbrier Mountain, an awesome setting for a round of golf. The most interesting hole is the 187-yard, par-3 8th. It is an excellent illustration of MacDonald's philosophies of natural design and bunker placement. It is similar to the 15th hole, called the Redan hole, at North Berwick, Scotland. The hole features a shallow, tilted green that swings around a deep bunker. Another bunker lies in wait behind the green. The bunkers

make an accurate tee shot essential because, if it lands in the front bunker, the recovery shot may flip over the green into the back bunker and set up a triple bogey.

A creek winds through the course but poses no major threat. MacDonald's philosophy of natural design opposed creating ponds and re-routing creeks. Water does come into play on the 417-yard 16th hole, a par 4. The hole has two greens. If the pin is located on the right green, the creek is off to the left. But, if it is set up on the left green, the hole becomes a dogleg, and the approach shot has to clear the creek. The toughest hole on the course is the 6th hole, a 444-yard par 4. It is a long hole with an out-of-bounds area to the right, and it runs uphill to the green. It's easy to miss the green, and bogeys are common. All holes are natural designs reflecting the philosophy Mac-Donald established as the father of American golf-course architecture.

If you don't carry the creek on the par-3 18th, your round is shot.

Charles Blair MacDonald transformed golf course design into an art.

HARLESTON GREEN

American golfers owe a great debt to Scotsmen, who were responsible for bringing the game to America. Golf had its beginnings in 16th-century Scotland and was exclusive to it until the 17th century when it traveled to England. Finally, in the late 18th century, it made its way to Charleston, South Carolina. Its first U.S. appearance was at Harleston Green, a field between downtown Charleston and the Ashley River. Today, the site is home to a Coast Guard base. Although it no longer exists, its heritage is preserved by the nearby Country Club of Charleston, which claims Harleston Green as its predecessor.

Most of the Scots in Charleston were merchants who traded goods with Glasgow. In the 1740s, longing to play their beloved native game, they began importing golf clubs and balls from Glasgow. They gathered in the field at Harleston Green and played much the same as they did at home. For the next forty years, golf was played at Harleston Green, and, in response to the game's popularity, the South Carolina Golf Club was formed in 1786. But, because this was just a few years after the American Revolution and golf was associated with the British, interest in golf waned. When the War of 1812 began, the game disappeared and Harleston Green was converted to a military base.

This tournament medal and original golf ball are sacred reminders of the first golf club in America.

HARLESTON GREEN

•

OAKHURST LINKS

•

no longer exist

This field in White Sulpher Springs was the site of Oakhurst Links.

OAKHURST LINKS

Americans went without golf for seventy years. It was revived in the 1880s in the wake of a golf boom in Scotland and England. Many players from these two countries immigrated to the U.S. to acquire land and earn tax-free money. Meanwhile, Americans who were educated in Scotland and England were discovering the game. One such American was Russell Wortley Montague, an 1874 Harvard graduate who went to Scotland to study international law. While he was there, his passion for golf developed on the Old Course at St. Andrews. When he returned home in 1878, he purchased the Oakhurst estate near White Sulphur Springs, West Virginia.

Down the road from his estate lived a Scotsman named George Grant, a retired British Army officer who had moved to White Sulphur Springs to enjoy the mineral-water baths at The Greenbrier Resort. In 1884 Grant's nephew, Lionel Torrin, told his uncle that he planned to visit him in the United States and wanted to bring his clubs. Because there would be no where for him to play, Grant approached Montague about building a golf club. When Torrin, who was an avid golfer, arrived in the spring, the three men laid out a 6-hole course on Montague's 60-acre estate. Alexander McLeod and Roderick McIntosh McLeod, two Scottish brothers who lived near the Oakhurst estate, took advantage of the opportunity to play their native game. Together, these five men formed the first golf club in America, Oakhurst Links.

Because the men had to make use of whatever equipment they could find, the course was rather primitive. The cups were simply tin cans sunken into the soil. The first tee sat atop a hill near Montague's home; the green was at the bottom of the hill. The second hole turned back and went up and over the hill alongside the house. The other four holes worked their way back and forth over the flat field below. Caddies were available to carry the usual six clubs. They were local kids who were making

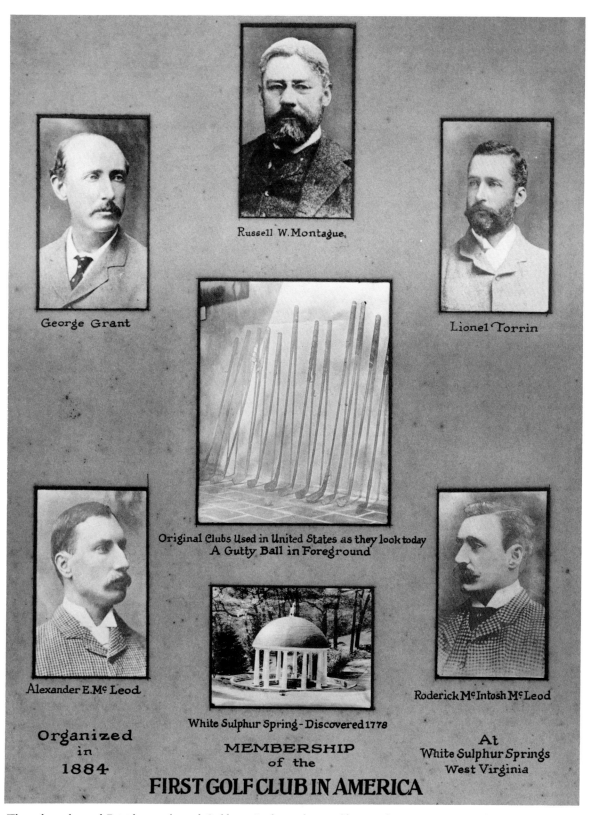

Russell W. Montague.

George Grant

Lionel Torrin

Original Clubs Used in United States as they look today
A Gutty Ball in Foreground

Alexander E. Mc Leod

White Sulphur Spring - Discovered 1778

Roderick McIntosh McLeod

Organized
in
1884

MEMBERSHIP
of the

At
White Sulphur Springs
West Virginia

FIRST GOLF CLUB IN AMERICA

These five relocated British men formed Oakhurst Links so they could enjoy their native game in the U.S.

The Oakhurst clubhouse, built in 1884, has been restored to its original condition.

quite a bit of money at 25 cents per round. The original greenskeepers were grazing sheep, but they couldn't keep up and members began losing balls in the deep grass. The sheep were soon replaced by Montague and a mechanical mower he was able to borrow from The Greenbrier. This was a significant improvement for the members who played with only one ball each round. If the ball disappeared in the tall grass, play stopped until it was found. If it couldn't be found, the round was over.

George Donaldson, another Scotsman, joined the club and took it upon himself to bring more clubs and balls from Scotland. When he was passing through U.S. customs on a return trip, an agent, who had never seen a golf club or even heard of the game, seized the clubs and accused Donaldson of smuggling a new type of murder weapon into the United States. "There is no such game played with such elongated blackjacks or implements of murder," he declared. It took the Treasury Department three weeks to confirm that there was a game called golf in Scotland, and the clubs were eventually returned to Donaldson with no apology. The first clubs all came from Scotland,

but a local man was taught how to make them to supplement the imports. Montague said the clubs were "pretty good, though not nearly as good as the real thing, which came from the forges of the St. Andrews, Scotland, area."

Oakhurst Links was an informal golf club, with only a clubhouse and six members. But the enthusiasm of those six members was great because they were playing the game they loved on the only course in the country. Every Christmas the club staged a match-play competition called the Challenge Medal. The medal, made by the Connecticut firm of Dieges and Clust, was engraved with the words "Oakhurst Links" and the classic Scottish golf motto "Far and Sure." In 1936, Montague told a reporter for the *Williamson News*, in West Virginia, "'Far and Sure' was an excellent motto, but not appropriate for us as none of us were very sure and we certainly did not drive very far." The Challenge Medal competition is often considered the first organized tournament in the United States.

During the recession of 1893 five of the original members left the U.S. Torrin and Grant moved to London and the McLeod brothers and Donaldson returned home to Scotland. Roderick McLeod left Oakhurst as the final winner of the Challenge Medal. After the other members left, Montague moved to Richmond, Virginia, and only returned to Oakhurst in the summers. The abandoned course returned to its natural state by 1900. Montague continued to enjoy golf by playing The Greenbrier until his death in 1945 at the age of 92. Even though Oakhurst Links no longer exists (though the current owner of the land is considering reconstructing the original course), it is still considered the first golf club in the United States.

Bobby Jones won his 1930 Grand Slam U.S. Open at Interlachen Country Club. Coincidentally, this is the only Open Interlachen has ever hosted, making Jones and the 1930 Open even more dear to the club and its members. Jones is remembered everyday at Interlachen through a drawing of him on the cover of their scorecard. Jones had always dreamed of winning the U.S. and British Opens and Amateurs in the same year, but the Grand Slam eluded him until 1930. He had won the U.S. Open, U.S. Amateur, and British Open but never the British Amateur. Jones felt confident that he could win the three tournaments he had already won again. So, if he could capture the British Amateur victory, he could win the Grand Slam of golf.

That year, Jones traveled to Britain as a member of the U.S. Walker Cup team. The team's win must have brought him luck, because he went on to win his first British Amateur, defeating Roger Wethered, the top Scottish player, 7 and 6 on St. Andrews's Old Course. Jones followed this victory by clinching his third career British Open at Hoylake. He then boarded the S.S. Europa and sailed to New York where Mayor Jimmy Walker threw a ticker tape parade to celebrate his wins. Jones was honored by the gesture, but his thoughts were on the Grand Slam. Eight days later he took his next step toward winning it at Interlachen.

Jones was playing well, but the great Walter Hagen was in the field. He would have to play at his best to win the third leg of the Grand Slam. The temperature the first day was 95 degrees and humidity was high, but the Southerner was used to playing in hot, sticky weather

INTERLACHEN COUNTRY CLUB

•

Edina, Massachusetts

•

6,804 yards, par 73

•

Designed by
William Watson

•

Redesigned by Donald Ross

and easily posted a 71. When he walked off the elevated 18th green, the spectators were taken aback by his appearance. Jones was soaked. His light gray knickers were stained red by the tees in his pockets; his white shirt was stained red from his tie; and his tie was so soggy that he couldn't even untie it. Atlanta journalist O.B. Keeler had to cut Jones's tie off with his pocket knife.

The 71 looked like it would be the lead, but later in the afternoon Macdonald Smith and Tommy Armour tied for the lead with 70. In the second round, a strong eastern wind brought the temperature down. Jones made the most memorable U.S. Open birdie in that round—mostly due to luck. The par-5 9th was

The only Grand Slam U.S. Open was won at Interlachen in 1930 by Bobby Jones.

485 yards with a large pond in front of the green. Jones hit a nice drive down the right side of the fairway. A 3-wood shot over the water should have put him on the green in two. Jones was in the middle of his backswing when two little girls ran onto the fairway. They interrupted his concentration, and he topped the ball. Amazingly, it skipped across the pond and landed on the bank. Using his wedge, Jones lofted the ball four feet from the cup and tapped in for birdie. Luck was definitely with Jones that day because, if the ball had splashed down, he would have been looking at a double bogey. He posted a second-round 73 to tie for second two strokes behind Horton Smith. Hagen was five strokes off Smith.

The third round set up Jones's Grand Slam Open victory. He shot an incredible 68, becoming the first golfer in U.S. Open history to break 70. He got down in two from a bunker for a birdie on the par-5 4th hole and birdied 6 and 7 to post a 33 on the front nine. Jones had back-to-back birdies on the par-5 11th and 12th holes and appeared to be headed for a 66. Unfortunately, he posted a pair of bogeys on the 17th and 18th to settle for a 68. That was good enough for a 5-stroke lead going into the fourth round that afternoon.

Jones was holding steady with a front-nine 38, but the field closed in on him when he double bogeyed the 194-yard, par-3 13th. Birdies on 14 and 16 balanced out the double bogey, but he posted another one on the par-3 17th when his tee shot landed in the water. Macdonald Smith was playing an excellent round and came within one stroke of Jones. Jones was headed for a bogey on the difficult 18th hole after his approach shot barely made it up the hill and onto the green. He was facing a 40-foot putt. Jones pulled out his prized putter, "Calamity Jane," and stroked the ball up the hill.

The ball broke right, spun toward the cup, and dropped in for a birdie. Jones won by two strokes with a final-round 75, his highest in the Open. Still, his 287 was his lowest U.S. Open score and brought him one step closer to the Grand Slam. Ten weeks later Jones won the U.S. Amateur at Merion to become the only Grand Slam winner in the history of golf.

THE COURSE

Interlachen demands perfect tee shots followed by perfect second shots. Donald Ross, taking advantage of the hilly landscape, laid out the fairways up and down slopes and designed holes so that the slopes would kick an off-line shot into a bunker or water hazard. Interlachen's greens may very well have been the smallest in U.S. Open his-

▶ *It takes a great drive to reach the 18th green at Interlachen.*

▼ *Bobby Jones skipped a ball across the pond on 9 and onto the green for a birdie in the 1930 U.S. Open.*

Tee shots landing on Interlachen fairways often kick off into the rough.

tory. In addition to the difficult size, an approach shot that isn't right on target tends to bounce off a green and into a hazard.

Golfers encounter Ross's slopes early in a round. The 351-yard, par-4 2nd hole may look easy on the scorecard, but bogeys are quite common. The fairway slopes to the left toward a tough bunker that snares many tee shots, making par nearly impossible. The 530-yard, par-5 4th hole presents the same problem, except that this sloping fairway directs shots into a pond to the right of the green instead of a sand trap.

This design makes distance off the tee less important than accuracy in the fairway. Many golfers at Interlachen will hit an iron off the tee to avoid bouncing off of a slope and into trouble. This is definitely the strategy to use on the 520-yard, par-5 9th hole, which is guarded by the pond that Jones skipped his ball across. Smart golfers will hit a fairway wood or long iron off the tee to land short of the pond and set up a reasonable second shot away from the water.

The slopes on the back nine are even tougher. For example, the 476-yard, par-5 11th hole looks like an eagle hole because of the length. But the fairway slopes about five different directions and sends many shots into the trees or bunkers, making par an admirable score. The 16th hole, a 318-yard par 4, is ranked as the easiest on the course, but the dogleg left can cause serious problems. Golfers who use a driver off the tee will hit through the fairway and end up chipping out of the woods. A solid iron tee shot will open up a playable approach shot, as long as it clears the six bunkers surrounding the small, elevated green. The ultimate elevated green is on the 400-yard, par-4 18th hole. The tiny green sits atop a high mound in front of the clubhouse. Most approach shots either kick off the hill into a bunker or leave a blind pitch shot. Donald Ross was surely proud of this green.

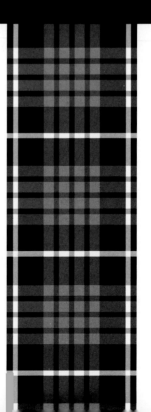

THE HISTORY

Inverness has hosted seven major championships since it opened in 1903. Although there are courses in the U.S. that have hosted more than seven majors, those staged at Inverness are among the most unique ever played. The first major staged at the club was the 1920 U.S. Open. The USGA was drawn to the course after Donald Ross officially designed and expanded it to 18 holes in 1919. This tournament started the trend of unique majors at Inverness.

The fact that this was Bobby Jones's first U.S. Open is not what made the major unusual. What made it unusual was Ted Ray's first and only U.S. Open victory. Ray, along with Harry Vardon, had lost the famous 1913 U.S. Open playoff to Francis Ouimet at Brookline. The 43-year-old was pitted against Vardon, 50, again in the 1920 U.S. Open. In the third round, Vardon was leading by one stroke over Jock Hutchison and Leo Diegel; Ray was two strokes back. A front-nine 36 followed by a par on 10 and a birdie on 11 gave Vardon a five-stroke lead with only seven holes to go. Suddenly, strong winds blew in off Lake Erie and the sky darkened. The change in weather brought about Vardon's demise. He wasn't as strong as Ray, and it took him four shots just to get on the 12th green. He followed the double bogey on 12 with a missed 2-foot par putt on 13. His collapse continued as he 2-putted 14, 15, and 16 and bogeyed 17 after his second shot splashed down. He was able to par 18 for a back-nine 42, but it wasn't enough. The wind had hindered Ray too, but he managed a back-nine 40. With his front-nine 35, he defeated Vardon by three strokes for his only U.S. Open victory. Eighteen-year-old Bobby Jones survived the stormy final round with a 77 to finish tied for eighth.

INVERNESS CLUB

•

Toledo, Ohio

•

7,025 yards, par 71

•

Designed by Donald Ross

•

Redesigned by
George and Tom Fazio

The longest playoff in U.S. Open History took place at Inverness in 1931. Billy Burke, a pro from Cleveland, and George Von Elm, an amateur from California, were tied at 292 after Von Elm sunk a 10-foot birdie putt on 18. Von Elm sunk another birdie putt on 18 to end the 36-hole playoff in a tie. The USGA called for a second 36-hole playoff. Von Elm led by a stroke after the 18th hole of the second playoff. But when they returned to the 18th to play the final playoff hole Burke had gained a 2-stroke lead, so even a biride couldn't save Von Elm. After an exhausting Open, the USGA limited the playoffs to 18 holes, with sudden death in the event of a tie.

The 1957 Open at Inverness was largely uneventful; Dick Mayer defeated Cary Middlecoff in an 18-hole playoff. In 1973, Inverness hosted the U.S. Amateur, which was won by Craig Stadler. After the Amateur, the USGA wanted to bring the Open back to the club in 1979. Inverness hired George Fazio and his nephew, Tom, to redesign the course. Hale Irwin won the 1979 Open on the newly designed course but only by the skin of his teeth. He had a solid 5-stroke lead over Jerry Pate and Gary Player until he double bogeyed 17 and bogeyed 18. His two strokes were still a win, but it was one of the worst finishes in U.S. Open history.

Even the great Byron Nelson has had a unique experience at Inverness. It came when he was playing in the Inverness Four-Ball in the 1930s paired with Walter Hagen. Hagen, in his 40s, considered Nelson, in his 20s, just a kid. After nine holes, Hagen was tired and stepped into the clubhouse to rest, letting Nelson play the best ball by himself. Hagen rejoined Nelson on the 14th tee, which is conveniently near the clubhouse. Even though

Ted Ray won his only U.S. Open at Inverness in 1920.

Hagen and Nelson were both great golfers, no one can win a best-ball tournament by himself. In fact, the pair finished last; that was the only time Nelson ever finished last in a tournament.

Inverness was good to Nelson. After he won the 1939 U.S. Open at Philadelphia Country Club, they hired him on as their head pro. This was a lucky break for Nelson, because tournament purses weren't enough to live off back then. Nelson says of the experience, "It was a great job for me because Inverness had a very full and active membership. It was the first club I was at where I really made some good money. The membership supported me very well. [Louise and I] started saving money for the first time."

If the Inverness gods were on Ted Ray's side in 1920, they were certainly against Greg Norman in 1986 and 1993. There have been two PGA Championships at the club, and Norman lost both of them on the 354-yard, par-4 18th hole—the shortest final hole in a major championship. Bob Tway defeated Norman in the 1986 PGA by hitting the greatest winning shot in the history of the PGA. At the turn, Tway was four strokes back, but he slowly closed in on Norman. On the 18th Tway holed out of the bunker in front of the green for a birdie and a one-stroke victory.

In the 1993 PGA, 18 knocked Norman out again. He was tied with Azinger on the final hole when he missed a 15-foot birdie that would have given him the win. Unfortunately for Norman, the sudden-death playoff began on the dreaded 18th. As if it was an instant replay,

Norman's approach shot landed just where it had before, and he missed the putt again. Norman and Azinger both parred and moved on to the 10th hole where Norman missed a 4-foot par putt to give Azinger his first major championship win. Coincidentally, in both 1986 and 1993, Norman had won the British Open just before playing the PGA at Inverness. Majors at Inverness provide golfers with extremes—either the best day of their life or the worst.

THE COURSE

Byron Nelson loves Inverness not just because the club has been so good to him but also because of the quality of the course itself. "I have always felt Inverness is a great golf course," he said. "The thing that makes it so great is the fairways are reasonably narrow and there is always good rough. The bunkers are really well done. The greens are small and you have to hit the ball straight to have good targets. There is such a variety of shots there."

Greg Norman lost the 1986 and 1993 PGAs on the 18th green at Inverness.

The scattered ponds make hitting a green at Inverness a formidable task.

the entire right side of the fairway, causing tee shots that go slightly too far right to get wet. The left side of the fairway isn't much more forgiving with its lining of thick trees. The creek runs all the way up to the green, and efforts to bail out often land in one of two bunkers on the left side of the green. Many golfers blast out of the bunkers too hard, rolling off the sloped, Donald Ross green and into the creek. Double bogeys are common on this hole, even more so than the par-4 7th.

The ubiquitous creek reappears on this 454-yard hole, swirling across the fairway and following it down the right side. Pushed tee shots have to carry 232 yards to clear the water. Even straight tee shots are in danger of taking a dip, because the creek creeps back toward the fairway to narrow the landing area. The green is elevated, so, whether it's the third, fourth, or fifth shot, the approach shot must land below the pin to leave a makeable putt.

The toughest hole on the back nine is the 448-yard, par-4 14th. It, too, demands a well-placed tee shot. The hole is similar to a dogleg right, requiring a tee shot to go down the left side of the fairway to set up an approach shot. A tee shot that goes too far left can land in the beach. Of course, the Ross green is small and protected by three menacing sand traps. This hole can make or break a back nine. In the final round of the 1993 PGA, Norman left his bunker shot in the bunker on the 210-yard, par-3 6th hole and double bogeyed as a result. If one of the world's best players leaves bunker shots in Inverness traps, so will most golfers.

Inverness definitely requires a wide range of shots. It is possible to hit a tee shot in the fairway and not have a clear shot to the green. The 409-yard, par-4 5th hole is a prime example of the importance of a proper tee shot. The hole doglegs left, so the tee shot has to be down the right side to open up the approach shot. Of course, there's a catch. A creek runs along

Tight fairways allow only exceptionally accurate golfers to win at Inverness.

I nwood Country Club, near JFK Airport on Long Island, has hosted only two major championships, but each brought an important victory for one of the two best American golfers of the early 20th century. Bobby Jones captured his first career U.S. Open in 1923 at Inwood and went on to win three more. Walter Hagen, already the titleholder of two U.S. Opens, won his first PGA Championship in 1921 at Inwood, going on to win four more.

Jones was well-known long before Inwood because of his charity work during World War I. As a teenager, he had put on golf exhibitions to raise funds for the Red Cross and War Relief. Although famous, Jones was frustrated by his losses at major tournaments. Before Inwood, Jones had played in ten British and U.S. national championships but had never won. The year before, Jones tied for second in the U.S. Open at Skokie, one stroke behind Gene Sarazen. Finally, his career took a sharp turn for the better at Inwood. But his victory wasn't guaranteed, and the 21-year-old struggled to the end. He took the third-round lead on Saturday morning, even though he shot a 76. In the final round, Jones appeared headed for a runaway victory. He was even par after 15 holes and three strokes ahead of Bobby Cruickshank, an excellent Scottish golfer. All Jones had to do was coast to the clubhouse. Instead, he bogeyed the par-4 16th and 17th holes. Still, he was in position to win if he could par the 18th.

That seemed easy enough. Jones had two birdies and a par on 18 in the first three rounds. He hit a good tee shot and chose a 2-wood for his second shot to overcome a strong wind in his face. The shot sailed over a treacherous creek in front of the green only to pull to the

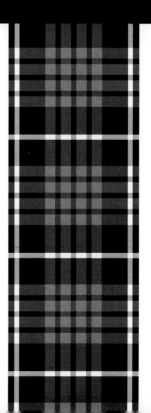

INWOOD
COUNTRY
CLUB

•

Inwood, New York

•

6,647 yards, par 72

•

Designed by
Herbert Strong

•

Redesigned by
Hal Purdy and Frank Duane

Bobby Cruickshank, who challenged Bobby Jones throughout the 1923 U.S. Open, surprised the world of golf when he birdied the 18th on the final day to force a playoff.

a two-stroke lead, but Cruickshank caught him by the 15th. Jones took the lead again on 16 only to be tied by the Scotsman on 17. The 18th hole would determine the winner. Cruickshank, who had the honors, hooked his tee shot into the rough. With the wind in their faces and a creek in front of the green, the final hole was dangerous. Cruickshank decided to layup short of the creek and try to get down in two for par; Jones opted to go for broke. He pulled out a midiron and nailed it six feet from the cup. He had to settle for par after he two-putted, but that was good enough because Cruickshank double bogeyed. Jones's career soared after his victory at Inwood. Over the next seven years, he won major championships routinely.

Hagen didn't have to rely on 18 to save his victory in the 1921 PGA at Inwood. However, the way he played the 11th hole prompted Inwood to remodel 18, making it a bit tougher. While playing in early matches, Hagen would hit his tee shot on 11 down nearby 18th fairway to open up his approach shot to the green. The novel strategy upset the club's pros, who met in the grill room one night and complained about Hagen. Around midnight, they found some laborers to uproot a 15-foot willow, later dubbed "Hagen's Willow," on 16 and move it to 18 to block Hagen's cuts.

Hagen lost the 11th hole in the 36-hole final-round match against Long Jim Barnes, the winner of the first two PGAs in 1916 and 1919 (it wasn't played during World War I). Barnes birdied 11 and Hagen parred. That birdie gave Barnes a 1-up lead. Hagen won the next three holes to go 2-up but finished the first round 1-up. Barnes couldn't catch Hagen in the final round. The 3 and 2 win brought Hagen his first PGA title. For the rest of the decade Hagen dominated the PGA Championship.

left rough. He chopped the approach into a bunker, then made the green, and two-putted for a double bogey.

Cruickshank was one stroke behind Jones when he stepped up to the 18th tee. He followed a good drive with a midiron six feet from the cup. He rolled in the putt to tie Jones. Most folks figured Jones would be demolished on the 18-hole playoff the next day. Cruickshank posted three birdies in the first five holes; Jones made only one. Then Jones's fortune changed. By the 13th hole, he had taken

The historic Inwood clubhouse offers an inviting spot to relax after a round of golf.

THE COURSE

Inwood hasn't been remodeled, so anybody who plays the course faces many of the same obstacles that Jones and Hagen confronted.

At 6,647 yards, Inwood was an enormously long course during the hickory-shaft era. It is now more of a midlength course, with sand traps as the major hazard. The 3rd, 4th, and 5th holes are consecutive par 5s, and each has several fairway bunkers capable of snaring errant tee shots. But, because the holes aren't too long, staying out of the bunkers can lead to birdies.

Although Inwood sits next to Jamaica Bay, water poses few problems on the course. Water really comes into play for the first time on the 106-yard, par-3 10th hole. But the tee shot is a short iron, so only the worst shots splash down. The next water hole is the 408-yard, par-4 18th—Jones's salvation in the Open. The hole can ruin a good round if the approach shot is fat, thanks to the rock-line creek 10 feet in front of the green. Chances are good that golfers will earn their first penalty stroke on the final hole.

Trees wall the holes at Inwood but rarely create problems because of the generous-sized fairways. Only wild tee shots end up in the trees, but plentiful fairway bunkers keep golfers on their toes to the end.

(Left) *Bobby Jones carried the creek in front of the 18th green to win his first U.S. Open in 1923.*
(Right) *The first water hazard that golfers encounter at Inwood is on the par-3 10th hole.*

KANSAS CITY COUNTRY CLUB

•

Shawnee Mission, Kansas

•

6,672 yards, par 70

•

Designed by
A.W. Tillinghast

•

Redesigned by Bob Dunning
and Rees Jones

Tom Watson was the first Baby Boomer to become a golf superstar. His success can be traced in part to his father, Ray Watson, who was an excellent golfer and encouraged his sons to take up the game. Ray was a low-handicap golfer who played in three U.S. Amateurs, reaching the quarterfinals in one. When Ray introduced his eldest son, Ridge, to golf, Tom, who was three years younger, was eager to follow in his brother's footsteps.

Ray Watson was, and still is, a member of Kansas City Country Club in Shawnee Mission, a suburb of Kansas City. One hot summer evening when Tom was 6 years old, the entire Watson family went out to the practice green. Ridge had already been playing for some time, but this was Tom's introduction to the game. Ray gave his youngest son a cut-down putter and taught him the basics of putting and gripping. Tom immediately took to the game and became devoted for life.

"Over 90 percent of all golfers on the Tour got started in the game from their relatives, mostly their dads," Tom once said. But not all fathers play as well as Ray Watson, who taught his sons how to play golf properly. When Tom was young, his father gave him lessons with a cut-down 5 iron. As he got older, he took lessons from club pro Stan Thisk. Fortunately, Kansas City Country Club did not place many restrictions on children playing the course. "Not that many people played the game and the course was basically ours, although there were restrictions in times," Watson recounts. "I remember days when I would go out there and play 36 holes, have a baloney sandwich, stop for lunch in the middle, and take a bottle of coke with me."

In addition to developing his playing prowess at an early age, Tom also learned to play competitively by going head to head with Ridge. "I am very competitive. We started to play and I always wanted to play against him. We played a lot of golf together at Kansas City Country Club," Watson said. Paul Weiler, another club pro, would pair younger and older kids in junior golf matches; Tom lost to Ridge in one of those tournaments. "Paul was instrumental in making me competitive," Watson said.

At age 12, Tom broke 80 for the first time, shooting a 76 at Kansas City Country Club.

The next year he broke 70. Because he was such an accomplished golfer at such an early age, Tom became friends with many pros around the Kansas City area. They often invited the fourteen-year-old to play golf with them on Mondays, their day off. The teenager improved his already excellent golf game by playing with the club pros. Tom won the Kansas City Men's Match Play Championship that year and was runner-up to his father in the Kansas City Country Club Championship. A few years later, he defeated his father to win the club championship.

THE COURSE

Thanks to Kansas City Country Club, Watson learned to chip well, which later became a key to his 1982 U.S. Open victory. The Kansas City course, although not dramatically long, has several greens that are either small or surrounded by grassy banks. This makes it easy for a good approach shot to miss the green. Watson learned this lesson at an early age and compensated by mastering his chip shot. "I would go around hitting four or five greens and shoot 78 or 75. There were push-up greens, so if you missed the greens, you had to learn to chip," Watson said. A chip shot on the 17th hole at Pebble Beach gave Watson his only U.S. Open title.

The 391-yard, par-4 1st hole at Kansas City Country Club warns golfers that they must chip

Tom Watson broke 80 for the first time at Kansas City Country Club when he was just twelve years old.

▲ *Finishing with a good score at KCCC requires avoiding the thick 18th-green sand trap.*

▶ *The dense trees lining the fairways forced Tom Watson to become a straight hitter.*

well to post a decent score. The hole runs downhill to a tiny green surrounded by four sand traps and thick grass, making chip shots almost a foregone conclusion. There are no water hazards to contend with on the front nine. Walnut trees, usually only about 50 yards in front of a green, replace water as a major hazard. They tend to block approach shots, but a good chip shot can get a golfer out of a jam. The 429-yard, par-4 4th hole is the most difficult on the course. It plays uphill off the tee and cuts many tee shots short. It takes a 260-yard tee shot to get over the rise and set up a reasonable approach shot.

Water does come into play on the back nine. Brush Creek hugs the right side of the fairway on the 398-yard, par-4 13th. Even though the hole is straight down the middle, the creek curls in front of the green, making it difficult to clear the water in two. It's not an impossible task, but a fat shot splashes down every time.

The 440-yard, par-4 16th hole is dry, but the green is still difficult to reach because it sits atop a hill. Many golfers hit a long iron or fairway wood on their second shot to avoid hitting the bank and kicking off into a bunker or onto the fringe. Poor scores on 13 and 16 can be erased on the 374-yard, par-4 18th, a simple hole to birdie. Many golfers revive their rounds on the final hole.

G olf fans are usually surprised to learn that Knollwood Country Club is the birthplace of the Masters. It was at this New York club that the concept of Augusta National was introduced by Bobby Jones. In fact, the Masters Tournament and Augusta National probably would not have been formed if it hadn't been for Knollwood.

It all began in the 1920s with New York banker Clifford Roberts. As a member of Knollwood, he would drive up to the club, located just north of Manhattan, regularly to play golf. One of Roberts's fellow members and golfing partners was Walton Marshall. Marshall owned the Vanderbilt Hotel in New York and the Bon Air Vanderbilt Hotel in Augusta, Georgia. Bobby Jones was a frequent guest at both hotels, and Marshall came to know him quite well. Because Roberts had long admired the esteemed golfer, Marshall introduced the two. Robert and Jones came to know each other well, because they both sought refuge from the cold New York winters by traveling south to play golf at Augusta Country Club.

In 1929, Roberts invited Jones to play in a four-ball match at Knollwood. Jones struggled a bit on the front nine but played well on the back. He shot a 2-under 68—par was 70 back then—to set a course record that lasted until Mike Turnesa shot a 64 in 1935. Jones and Roberts had become good friends by that time, and Jones told Roberts of his plan to form a private club in Augusta. He envisioned it as a winter golf vacation spot for affluent northeastern golfers. Jones met with Roberts again at Knollwood after winning the 1930 Grand Slam and announcing his retirement from golf. This time he was ready to plan the details of his Augusta course.

KNOLLWOOD COUNTRY CLUB

•

Elmsford, New York

•

6,410 yards, par 71

•

**Designed by
Lawrence Van Etten**

Lawrence Van Etten designed the original layout, which lasted until the mid-1920s.

Augustus T. Gillender (left) began planning Knollwood in 1890.

When The House was built in 1892, the south wing had yet to be built.

He invited Alister MacKenzie, the English golf-course architect who designed Cypress Point Golf Club in Monterey, California, to join him and Roberts in a round of golf. Jones had enjoyed playing Cypress Point in 1929 and felt that MacKenzie was the best candidate to design his golf course. At the time the three men were discussing the new course, the Great Depression was just beginning. Although they felt the Depression would end shortly, they were concerned about creating a national private club when their potential affluent members were losing their money. Upon finishing the round, the three men retired to the Grill Room where they worked out the possible problems facing Augusta National and devised a concrete plan.

MacKenzie was impressed with the 19th hole, called the "Bye Hole," at Knollwood, and

included one in his original design of Augusta National. It was to be similar to the Bye Hole, running uphill to the clubhouse from the 18th green. Ultimately, Jones decided not to include the 19th hole. However, the brainstorming that Roberts, Jones, and MacKenzie did at Knollwood led to the birth of Augusta National and the Masters.

THE COURSE

Knollwood's course is much the same as it was in the days of Jones and Roberts. The only major changes have been to the 365-yard, par-4 1st hole and the 390-yard, par-4 2nd hole. When the state of New York built the Tappen Zee Bridge across the Hudson River and extended the Cross Westchester Expressway, a road was constructed on top of the

The last hole at Knollwood, the 19th going toward the clubhouse, is the "Bye Hole."

Knollwood is a roller-coaster golf course with its steep up-and-down fairways.

Hitting the 18th green in regulation is difficult because of the trees and water that must be avoided.

original first green and second tee. The new holes embrace the original design as much as possible, but they did lose some length.

Golfers have to stay on their toes to score well at Knollwood. Because the fairways are a bit narrow, tee shots and approach shots must be long and straight. This is especially true of the 420-yard, par-4 6th hole, which doglegs right around a group of trees and has a large bunker in front of the green. Many golfers end up chipping out of the trees and facing a long third shot just to save bogey. The next hole, a 373-yard par 4, features the course's first water hazard, a pond just in front of the green. Slicers will post a penalty stroke.

The 289-yard, par-4 14th is perhaps the easiest hole in Westchester County. It is a slight dogleg left, and most golfers get close to the green off the tee. It is important to birdie 14, because the 437-yard, par-4 18th often costs a stroke. It is a potentially disastrous hole that doglegs right with an extensive carry over water. It is possible to land the tee shot far down the fairway if it's hit off a high tee. Even when this miracle occurs, you have to be in just the right location, left of center in the fairway, to hit your second shot over the water and through the trees. Many a ball has been lost after bouncing off a tree and into the water.

After surviving the terrifying 18th hole, playing the 123-yard, par-3 Bye Hole is a delight. In fact, members often make small wagers to make the hole more exciting. All it takes is a short iron over a small pond to birdie the hole. For many guests at Knollwood, it is the first, and probably only, time they birdie a 19th hole.

Arnold Palmer was extremely lucky to be born the son of a professional golfer on September 10, 1929. His dad, Milfred "Deacon" Palmer, was head pro and greenskeeper at Latrobe Country Club, located in the Western Pennsylvania town of Latrobe fifty miles east of Pittsburgh. Because his dad was a golf pro, Arnie was introduced to golf at a young age. Golf quickly became the foundation of his life, and he was able to develop his golf game before he was ten years old. With golf as the focus of his life so early, Palmer was destined to become the "King of Golf."

Arnie set out for his crown at age five. His parents lived in a house next to the 5th tee of what was then a 9-hole golf course. Being able to look outside and see people playing golf naturally drew Arnie to the game. He started with a cut-down ladies' iron. "Pap," Arnie's nickname for his dad, spent a lot of time teaching him how to get the right start in golf. Pap emphasized teaching his son the proper grip; he always felt that the key to being a successful golfer was having a good grip. Pap also believed that ninety percent of golf is played from the shoulders up, so he taught Arnie to combine mental attitudes with the techniques of a good golf swing.

When Palmer got older, he became a caddie master at Latrobe. One of the club members joked that he was a bad caddie master because he was such a good golfer. Palmer often played the 9-hole course by himself. He made a game of playing four balls on each hole. He'd dedicate each ball to one of the great players of the decade, the 1940s: Byron Nelson, Ben Hogan, Sam Snead, and Jug McSpaden. Because Nelson was the best player of that era, the Nelson ball always beat the other three balls.

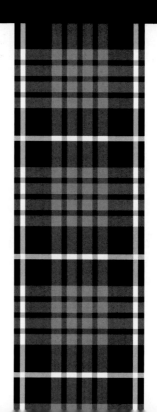

LATROBE COUNTRY CLUB

•

Latrobe, Pennsylvania

•

6,290 yards, par 72

•

Designed by Emil Loeffler
and John McGlynn

•

Redesigned by
James Gilmore Harrison

◀ *The tee for the par-3 10th hole is located at the top of a hill.*

▲ *Charles Funk, Babe Zaharias, Arnold Palmer, and Pat Harrington (left to right) look on as Dean Palmer tees off in a 1949 exhibition.*

▲ *Deacon Palmer, Arnold Palmer, and Club President Harry Saxman (left to right) oversaw the course expansion to 18 holes in the early sixties.*

Chestnut Ridge creates the wooded backdrop for the 18th green and the clubhouse.

The Latrobe High School golf team played at Latrobe Country Club. Before Palmer was even old enough to be in high school, he was playing golf with the team. He consistently beat the members of the team—by the time he was twelve years old he was already breaking 70.

When Arnie started high school, he was playing in local, state, and national tournaments. While playing in the National Hearst Junior, he met a guy named Bubby Worsham. Bubby convinced Arnie to go to Wake Forest University in North Carolina where the weather was warm all year round, unlike the icy cold winters on Latrobe. Bubby and Arnie were pals and played on the golf team together at Wake Forest. In 1950, their senior year, Bubby died in an auto accident. This had a dramatic impact on Arnie. He dropped out of Wake Forest and enlisted in the Coast Guard. While in the military, Palmer did play in some tournaments. When his tour of duty ended, he went back to Wake Forest and studied business administration.

Arnie left Wake Forest when he got a job in Cleveland as a manufacturer's representative. Fortunately, his boss was a golf enthusiast and encouraged him to play in tournaments. Palmer entered the 1954 U.S. Amateur at the Country Club of Detroit and defeated Robert Sweeny 1-up in the final to win his first national championship. A few months later he turned pro and started recruiting the crew of "Arnie's Army" by becoming the most talented and friendliest professional golfer at a time when tournaments were first being televised. Growing up next to the 5th tee at Latrobe Country Club and being the son of a great club pro, Arnold Palmer was fated to be golf's King.

THE COURSE

Anyone who plays Latrobe will instantly discover what made Arnold Palmer such a great go-for-broke golfer. Most of the original nine holes from Arnie's youth still exist, and the new nine is very similar. All 18 holes contain lush trees, rolling fairways, undulating greens, and scattered bunkers. Only six holes have water hazards that come into play. Arnie probably became a go-for-broke golfer because he grew up near the 439-yard, par-4 3rd hole. It's a sharp dogleg right with a large pond just past the corner of the dogleg. It requires a straight tee shot to set up a reasonable second shot over the water to the small green. Anyone who hit a mediocre tee shot would have to go for broke to clear the water.

The 490-yard, par-5 8th hole requires a similar strategy. It is short enough to hit in two. There are water hazards to both the right and left of the green. Golfers trying for an eagle have to hit a perfect second shot that goes straight at the green over the water. Hooks and slices splash down every time.

The 335-yard, par-4 12th hole looks short on the scorecard, but a creek crosses the fairway about 240 yards off the tee. A good golfer can try for the green by hitting over the water, leaving a flip wedge to the green. A conservative golfer can layup with a long iron and follow with a midiron shot to the green.

The tee shot on the 469-yard, par-5 14th hole is another sort of all-or-nothing shot. The creek that crosses 12 also traverses 14. It's not a long carry to the fairway; however, a tee shot that flies over the creek and goes left may kick out of bounds. Playing a round of golf at Latrobe Country Club makes a golfer realize how Arnie became the greatest go-for-broke golfer in the world.

▲ Arnold Palmer was practicing with the Latrobe High School golf team at Latrobe County Club before he was even old enough to join the team.

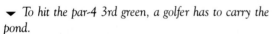

▼ To hit the par-4 3rd green, a golfer has to carry the pond.

Merion Golf Club is frequently considered the most historic golf course in the United States. It owes its fame to the United States Golf Association. Enamored with the East Course, the organization conducted 15 national championships there through 1989, including four U.S. Opens and five U.S. Amateurs. Two of these majors were pivotal in the careers of Ben Hogan and Bobby Jones. The 1950 U.S. Open was won by Hogan in a comeback after a near-fatal car accident, and Jones captured the 1930 Amateur to write the final chapter of his Gand Slam.

However celebrated, Merion is not likely to stage any more U.S. Opens. As excellent as the course is, it just doesn't have the space to accommodate the many corporate hospitality tents and huge numbers of cars that accompany modern Opens. "I guess it is kind of sad they will not go back for another Open," said David Graham, winner of the 1961 U.S. Open at Merion. "Certainly it is no fault of the golf course. The U.S. Open has grown so much in the past few years, they don't have the space."

At 6,482 yards, the East Course is probably the most challenging par 70 in the world. It is unfortunate that future Open players will miss the opportunity to play the magnificent course that has witnessed so many memorable moments in golf history. The U.S. Open has lost a great course.

Merion Cricket Club, as it was originally known, was formed in 1865 just after the Civil War. Golf wasn't popular in the U.S. at that time, but cricket was a favorite pasttime. Bobby Jones loved Merion. He won his first career U.S. Amateur in 1924 on the East Course, defeating George Von Elm 9 and 8 in the 36-

MERION GOLF CLUB, EAST COURSE

•

Ardmore, Pennsylvania

•

6,482 yards, par 70

•

Designed by Hugh Wilson

•

Redesigned by Bill Flynn and Perry Maxwell

hole final. When Jones returned to Merion in 1930, he was seeking the Grand Slam, having already won the U.S. Open, British Open, and British Amateur that year.

With the possibility of Jones clenching the Grand Slam, interest in the tournament was at a high. The USGA charged spectators one dollar to view practice rounds, and 4,000 people showed up to watch Jones prepare for the win. Jones shot a 73 in the first practice round and a 78 in the second, feeling the pressure as the

Ben Hogan won the 1950 U.S. Open in an amazing comeback from a nearly fatal car accident.

crowds closed in on him. He escaped to Pine Valley for one practice round, then returned the next day to Merion and shot a 74. He had planned to take the day off before the tournament, a regimen he always followed in major championships. He would stay in his hotel room, read a book, and relax. Unfortunately, USGA President Findlay Douglas pleaded with Jones to play another practice round because of the spectator fees he was pulling in. The USGA ultimately earned $55,000 in the 1930 U.S. Amateur, a great deal of money at that time.

Jones shot a 69 in the final practice round. During the qualifying round, the gallery swelled to 7,000 spectators, and almost all of them followed Jones. Merion provided him with 50 Marines as security guards. Jones shot 69-73—142 to win the medalist honor and tie the qualifying round. The year before, Jones lost in the first round of the Amateur at Pebble Beach. He was concerned about this first round because he was playing Sandy Somerville, a three-time winner of the Canadian Amateur. His worries didn't slow him down, because he shot a front-nine 32 and won the match 5 and 4. He kept up the streak, defeating 1922 Amateur champion Jess Sweetser 9 and 8 in the semifinals, thanks to five birdies on the last 10 holes.

Jones had to defeat Eugene Homans, a lanky golfer from New Jersey, to win the Grand Slam. The final match drew 18,000 spectators. This proved unsettling to Homans, who played six holes before making par. Down three to Jones, Homans parred the 7th and cut the lead to 2. Jones continued to play well and finished the first 18 holes 7-up. In the afternoon, Jones was 8-up after nine holes. On the 387-yard, par-4 11th hole, Jones was dormie 8. All he had to do was halve the hole for the Grand Slam. The green is surrounded by water, so Jones could still lose the hole. Both players hit good drives. Homans hit first and lofted a niblick 18 feet from the pin; Jones hit his niblick 20 feet from the hole. Jones stroked his putt within 10 inches of the hole, forcing Homans to sink his putt to keep the match going. After his putt broke off from the hole, he walked up to Jones with a smile, shook his hand, and conceded the putt. The crowd cheered wildly in honor of Jones's Grand Slam. No golfer has ever equalled Jones feat. The 11th hole marks the most celebrated event in the history of the East Course.

Bobby Jones celebrated the completion of his 1930 Grand Slam in the Merion clubhouse.

Ben Hogan signaled his full recovery after the car accident with his 1950 U.S. Open victory on the East Course. He approached the Open in his usual style, analyzing the course during practice. He concluded that he wouldn't need a 7-iron, so he tossed it from the bag and replaced it with a 1-iron to help him reach some of the long par 4s.

Lee Mackey, a driving range pro from Birmingham, Alabama, who won a playoff for the final qualifying position, shot a 6-under 64 in the first round to set a U.S. Open record and take the lead. The pressure proved too great for Mackey, however, and he slipped to an 81 in the second round. Mackey finished the tournament tied for 26th place.

Hogan posted a 69 in the second round, placing him in fifth behind Dutch Harrison, Johnny Bulla, Julius Boros, and Jim Ferrier. On the grueling final day, then consisting of 36 holes, Hogan moved up to a tie for third after a morning-round 72. He was two strokes behind 1946 U.S. Open Champion Lloyd Mangrum and one back from Harrison. In the afternoon, most of the contenders began to falter—except George Fazio, a former Canadian Open cham-

pion who would later earn a reputation as one of America's finest golf course architects, who posted a 70 to shoot 287. Mangrum began to slip and managed a 76 to tie Fazio. Hogan, who was on the 12th hole when Mangrum finished second, appeared to have the tournament in his pocket. All he needed was a two-over-par round to win. He bogeyed the 12th, then missed a three-foot par putt on 15. With three holes to go, he had to par in to win. He parred the 16th, the infamous quarry hole but dropped his tee shot on the par-3 17th in a bunker. He then missed a five-foot par putt to tie Mangrum and Fazio.

Hogan's par on the 458-yard 18th hole is legendary. He hit a solid drive down the middle to face a lengthy 1-iron shot to the green. The ball landed 40 feet from the cup, and he two-putted to tie Fazio and Mangrum, setting up an 18-hole playoff the next day. As Hogan walked off the green, an unknown fan stole the 1-iron from his bag. That was the last Hogan saw of it until 1983, when a golf collector who had purchased the MacGregor from an anonymous dealer returned it to him.

A drive hit from the back tee on 18 has to carry at least 210 yards just to reach the fairway.

During the playoff, Hogan was unbeatable. On the 16th green, Hogan was a stroke ahead of Mangrum and three ahead of Fazio. Mangrum faced a 12-foot par putt. Just as he was about to putt, a bug landed on his ball. He picked up the ball and blew the bug off. The USGA assessed Mangrum a two-stroke penalty for picking up the ball, clearing the way for Hogan's victory. A birdie on the 17th sealed his comeback with a 69.

THE COURSE

Merion's East Course, which has changed very little over the years, posed much the same challenges to Jones and Hogan as it did to Lee Trevino in 1972 and David Graham in 1981. "It is what we classify as an old-style, traditional course," Graham said. "Length is not a major criterion, shot placement is. The East Course is superbly bunkered. It is as good a design of putting surfaces as you could find anywhere. It's a thinking man's golf course—a classic, a jewel, fabulous."

The final three holes may be the finest of all. The 428-yard, par-4 16th green is perched atop a hill behind a quarry of water, bunkers, and trees. The tee also sits up high, leaving the fairway far below. Hitting toward the green off the tee puts the ball in deep rough. Golfers must also hit over the quarry on the 220-yard, par-3 17th. It is a downhill shot to a green surrounded by bunkers. "The 17th hole has to be one of the best par 3s in the world, and 18 has got to be one of the best finishing holes," Graham said. The 18th hole is 463 yards off the back tee, and the drive must carry 210 yards just to reach the fairway. The approach shot has to be right on line because shots to the left are likely to hit trees and bounce into the clubhouse parking lot. A good round can easily turn into a nightmare on the last three holes of the East Course.

Merion is considered an old-style course because shot placement is a greater factor than length.

To say that Byron Nelson's phenomenal year of 1945 will never be equalled is like saying no one will ever match Joe DiMaggio's 56-game hitting streak or Wilt Chamberlain's 100-point basketball game.

In 1945, Nelson won 18 tournaments and set the PGA Tour record of 11 consecutive wins. No one will even come close to this record. Nelson's detractors downplay his accomplishments, pointing out that it was wartime and that the PGA fields were largely made up of military rejects and has-beens too old to serve overseas. (Nelson couldn't serve because he was declared 4-F due to his hemophilia.) However, by mid-year the tour was back in full swing. Sam Snead had returned from the Navy after slipping a vertebra and Ben Hogan returned from the war that summer. Between the three of them, they captured 29 of the scheduled 35 events that year. Nelson started the year slowly, allowing Snead to steal the Los Angeles Open by one shot. He quickly bounced back with a victory at Phoenix and threw a pair of 269s at the field in Tucson and San Antonio, losing by a stroke to Ray Mangrum and Sam Byrd respectively.

Nelson got back on track with a 16-under-par 264 at Corpus Christi and followed with a win over Jug McSpaden in New Orleans. His bid for three in a row fell short at Gulfport when he lost to Snead in a sudden-death play-off. Snead went on a rampage of his own with back-to-back victories in Pensacola and Jacksonville for his third and fourth wins of the year.

Nelson's 11 consecutive wins began at the Miami International Four-Ball played at Miami Springs Country Club. There was little to indicate what lay ahead. Snead was the leading

MIAMI SPRINGS COUNTRY CLUB

•

Miami Springs, Florida

•

6,741 yards, par 71

•

**Designed by
Thomas "Tubby" Palmer**

money winner, having captured six events since his return to the tour in late 1944. All of that was to change at placid Miami Springs.

Nelson was teamed with his buddy, Mc-Spaden, and the pair played superbly in the match-play event. They were down only once in the four-day tournament—when Sammy Byrd, paired with Denny Shute, birdied the 2nd hole of the morning round. That wasn't good enough to defeat Nelson and McSpaden, who didn't record a single team bogey in the entire tournament. With Nelson's birdie on the 9th hole, the team posted a 30 and took a 2-up lead. Byrd swung back with a birdie on the 10th to cut the lead to 1-up. In the final round, Nelson and McSpaden birdied four of the first six holes to go 6-up, then cruised the course and won the match 8 and 7. The big victory inspired Nelson. "I became confident," Nelson said. "I realized I could do with the golf ball pretty much what I wanted to do."

The next week it was Greensboro, followed by Durham, then Atlanta—all victories for Nelson. The strain from winning was catching up with him. During a six-week lull in the tour, Nelson confided to his wife, Louise, that he

wished his streak would end. Instead, he headed back to the tour in June to carve out another streak of 66s and 67s. By then, he had broken Snead's record for the most wins in a season and was headed for the PGA Championship in Dayton, Ohio, in July.

But until Dayton, Nelson had to contend with the rising pressure to sustain "The Streak," as it was called in the newspapers. He took the Montreal Open by 10 shots to start the summer tour and followed with the *Philadelphia Inquirer* Invitational, closing with a 63 to beat McSpaden by two strokes and gain his seventh consecutive win.

In Chicago, he coasted to his eighth win by a seven-stroke margin. Nelson was ready to put the streak on the line at the PGA. By this time the specter of Snead had faded. Slammin' Sammy had broken a wrist sliding into second during a softball game at his home in Hot Springs, Virginia, and was out for the summer. But Nelson didn't need the long-hitting mountain man to spur his game.

The PGA meant more to Nelson than other tournaments. Nelson lost the PGA event the previous year to Bob Hamilton, an unknown

	PALM PASS	FICUS WAY	DISTANT GREEN	HIDDEN BROOK	PINECREST	SHERWOOD	HIGHLANDS	WATERWAY	SAND DUNES		TALL PINE	COURTYARD	BLACK FOREST	KING'S ALLEY	GRASSLANDS	BIRDIE LEFT	OAK'S JOURNEY	SABAL TRAIL	MELALEUCA MILE			USGA Course Ratings Blue: 71.0 White: 72.0 Red: 72.5	
HOLE	1	2	3	4	5	6	7	8	9	Out	10	11	12	13	14	15	16	17	18	In	Tot	Hdcp	Net
CHAMPIONSHIP	410	445	250	538	328	545	140	438	434	3528	403	367	403	178	505	337	430	220	370	3213	6741		
WHITE COURSE	390	436	242	528	317	530	136	428	413	3420	393	346	383	163	484	319	410	203	355	3056	6476		
HANDICAP	11	1	13	7	15	5	17	3	9		2	10	6	18	8	14	4	16	12				
PAR	4	4	3	5	4	5	3	4	4	36	4	4	4	3	5	4	4	3	4	35	71		
WON / LOST																							
RED COURSE	360	423	203	461	290	463	126	367	350	3043	382	324	363	149	454	301	295	186	339	2793	5836		
HANDICAP	11	7	17	1	9	3	15	5	13		2	10	4	18	6	12	16	14	8				
PAR	4	5	4	5	4	5	3	4	4	38	4	4	4	3	5	4	4	3	4	35	73		

Hurricane Andrew tore up some of Miami Springs' oldest trees.

army private, and he was determined to make amends. Match play, the format of the PGA in those years, allows little room for error. Unlike stroke play, in which a careless shot one day can be eclipsed by a brilliant one the next, match play ends with a loss. So an obscure player can upset a champion with a hot round, only to fade away the next day.

Nelson appeared headed for certain defeat in the PGA as he dueled with Mike Turnesa, a solid but unspectacular player from New York. Turnesa held a two-hole lead over Nelson with just four left to play in the second round. The 15th proved to be a turning point. Nelson closed birdie, birdie, eagle, par to win 1-up on the final green. The shell-shocked Turnesa, who had fired 68-69 in the 36-hole match, quipped, "How can you beat a guy like that?" Nelson calmly went about his business in the finals, whipping Byrd 4 and 3 for his fifth and last major title.

His 10th win came at the tour's richest tournament, the All-American Open at Chicago's Tam O'Shanter course. The 11th win came in the Canadian Open. His streak ended the next week in Memphis when New Orleans amateur Freddie Haas won the tournament and Nelson finished fourth. The ledger for 1945 was particularly impressive in light of the paltry purses common at the time. Nelson's $63,335.66 in earnings stood unchallenged for nine years, and no other golfer has ever won more than 13 tournaments in a single year. Nelson's worst finish of the year was a tie for 10th at Tacoma; he finished first or second in 25 out of 30 tournaments, and his 68.33 scoring average is still the lowest in PGA Tour history.

THE COURSE

Miami Springs is one of the best public golf courses in Florida. The front nine is about 2½ strokes more difficult than the back nine, mainly because of the 2nd and 3rd holes. The 2nd hole is a 445-yard, dogleg-right par 4. On the turn, the approach shot is usually into the wind. A good tee shot shoots past the corner of the dogleg and avoids a corner bunker. The second shot is 190 yards uphill, into the wind to the green. The golfer who

Miami Springs has been called the best public course in Florida.

The Miami Springs clubhouse is right on Red Road, across the street from the back nine.

escapes with a par or bogey faces a good chance of a double bogey on the 250-yard, par-3 3rd hole. Winds and cross winds are common, and the small green is easy to miss with a 3-wood or driver.

The 438-yard, par-4 8th hole, the 17th in Nelson's day, also plays into the wind. The fairway grass is thick, so drives don't run much. A creek crosses the fairway about 290 yards off the tee. Generally, only a John Daly-style golfer has to worry about the creek, although average golfers sometimes find trouble there. The creek curls to the right of the fairway, making slices perilous. To the left are palm trees, so the tee shot must be straight. Good golfers can easily carry the creek, but high handicappers often face a carry over the stream and a potential penalty stroke. The green is large, and three-putting is common.

The back nine is not as severe a test, but the 16th and 17th holes can be as problematic as 2 and 3. The 16th is a 430-yard dogleg-left par 4, a long and demanding hole in regulation play. The 220-yard, par-3 17th hole is uphill, and the green is guarded by bunkers. The only solution is a perfect tee shot. Luckily, golfers can recover on the wide fairway of the 370-yard, par-4 18th, a birdie hole.

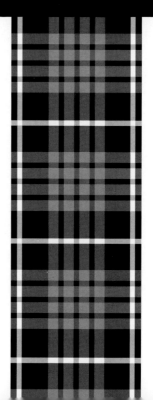

MIDLOTHIAN COUNTRY CLUB

•

Midlothian, Illinois

•

6,661 yards, par 71

•

Designed by H.J. Tweedie

•

Redesigned by Ken Killian and Dick Nugent

Walter Hagen is considered one of the best American golfers of the early 20th century. His golf career began as a caddie at his home course, the Country Club of Rochester, where he also turned pro. As a 21-year-old club pro, Hagen wasn't a golf enthusiast. His sport was baseball. He was a big fan of the game and badly wanted to play Major League Baseball. It's not surprising that baseball appealed to the young athlete. Players were making good money, much more than golf pros, and were popular with the public. Hagen did, however, play pro golf and did exceedingly well in his first U.S. Open in 1913. He finished tied for fourth at the famous Open at The Country Club at Brookline, just three strokes behind the tied Francis Ouimet, Harry Vardon, and Ted Ray.

Hagen was pleased with his performance but still not convinced that the world of golf was as exciting as the world of baseball. The following year, the U.S. Open was played at Midlothian Country Club in the South Chicago suburb of Midlothian. Hagen wasn't interested in leaving Rochester to play in the Open in Chicago. In his entire life, he had never left the northeast. One day, when he was hanging out in the pro shop, he bragged to Dutch Leonard about how well he was hitting the baseball. He had arranged a tryout with the Philadelphia Phillies in the 1915 spring training. Hagen was convinced he could become a big league player.

Ernest Willard, editor of the *Rochester Democrat and Chronicle,* came by the pro shop to pick up his clubs for a trip. As Hagen walked out to meet Willard, Leonard asked, "Aren't you going to enter the National Open at Chicago?" Hagen said he wanted to work harder on baseball and give up golf. Willard heard Hagen and tried to convince him that he had time to play golf and baseball. Willard wanted Hagen to go to the Open because he did so well at Brookline and the club was proud of him for becoming the first club pro to qualify for the Open. Willard even offered to pay Hagen's travel expenses if he entered the Open. The free trip finally convinced Hagen to enter. Still, he viewed the trip to Chicago more like a vacation than business.

Hagen and Leonard took a train to Chicago and checked into the Great Northern Hotel. After getting settled, he and Dutch went to an upscale restaurant and ate red lobster and oysters. Afterwards they went to a movie where Hagen started feeling sick to his stomach. When they returned to the hotel around midnight, Dutch called the hotel doctor who gave Hagen some pills, but Hagen couldn't keep them down. Hagen felt that he was too sick to play in the Open. After much persuading, Dutch convinced him to go out to Midlothian and play a practice round; he was worried Wil-

lard would be upset if Hagen withdrew completely. Hagen played fairly well in the practice round after the doctor gave him some milk toast and aspirin to relieve his pain. He then felt well enough to play in the first round.

He walked up to the 1st tee and hit a great shot over a pond to par the hole. Hagen continued playing well and finished with a course-record 68 to take the first-round lead. This was the first time a golfer shot in the 60s in the U.S. Open. Hagen changed his clothes and walked out to the front of the clubhouse to check the scoreboard. He was expected to have a big lead, so he was surprised to see that defending champion Francis Ouimet posted a 69. Hagen's confidence diminished because Ouimet was considered the best golfer in the country. Things looked better after the second round when Ouimet blew up to 76 and Hagen shot a 74 to maintain the lead.

A third-round 75 gave him a four-stroke lead over Charles "Chick" Evans, an amateur and Chicago native who won the Western Amateur. The gallery didn't show much interest in Hagen, following Evans in the final round. Ha-

Midlothian added several ponds to improve irrigation and make the 14th and 18th holes more difficult.

▲ *To reach this par-3 green, golfers must hit long and high.*

▶ *Midlothian comes alive with color each spring.*

gen shot a front-nine 38, and Evans, with his local fans in tow, shot a front-nine 35 to cut Hagen's lead to one stroke. Hagen kept hooking on the back nine but was successfully sinking recovery putts, such as a 12-foot par putt on the 13th hole. On the par-5 16th hole, Hagen pulled a 2-wood left of the green and duffed the pitch shot so that it barely reached the green. Amazingly, he rolled in a 40-foot birdie putt. He finished the round by sinking an eight-foot par putt on the 18th green to shoot a 73 and post a 72-hole 290.

Evans, trailing three holes behind Hagen, was playing well. He stepped up to the 18th tee two shots back. The 18th is a short par 4, so there was a chance Chick would eagle for a tie. Evans hit an excellent tee shot and lofted a niblick right at the hole. The ball hit the back of the hole but popped out and stopped a foot behind the cup, giving Hagen the win.

Once he had a taste of a national championship title, he decided that golf might just be a better sport than baseball, so he turned down the chance to try out for the Phillies and devoted his life to golf. If it hadn't been for the U.S. Open win at Midlothian, the world of golf may have lost Walter Hagen to baseball forever.

THE COURSE

Herbert James Tweedie's design of Midlothian is a perfect imitation of a Robert Trent Jones course. The 205-yard 2nd hole is a classic Trent Jones par 3. It is a long hole that plays into the wind, which makes it even longer. A large bunker in front of the green adds to the hole's difficulty. Members often settle for a 5-iron off the tee and pitch on for a one-putt par or two-putt bogey. Either way, it beats a double bogey after being buried in the sand. It's a tough par 3, but it at least allows for a bogey.

The 151-yard, par-3 12th hole usually leads to a double bogey, especially if the tee shot is off line. It's all carry over a rock-lined pond. It is easier, however, to clear the water with a 5-iron than to carry a bunker with a fairway wood or driver.

Water isn't a natural hazard in the wooded area south of Chicago. Midlothian added several ponds to improve irrigation and add difficulty to two short holes. One of these holes is the 316-yard, par-4 14th, which looks like a birdie hole on the scorecard.

One pond was added to the right side of the dogleg and another in front of the green where bunkers used to sit. Like the 14th hole, the 8th, a 319-yard par 4, can swallow off-line shots. A pond was built about 150 yards off the tee. A good tee shot to the left can avoid the water, but a slice will splash down every time. Midlothian's water hazards turn easy holes into rigorous ones.

Despite the water, the back nine is easier than the front nine. One reason is the sharply undulating front-nine greens; another is the additional 183 yards. The front-nine par is 35 with only one birdie par 5 compared to two birdie par 5s and two birdie par 4s on the par-36 back nine. There are also four par 4s over 400 yards on the front, including the longest on the course, the 439-yard 9th hole. Being a long hitter doesn't even help because two pit bunkers lie in wait 295 yards off the back tee. Boomers have to lay up to pull off a reasonable approach shot. It is holes like this that make Midlothian a traditional golf course Robert Trent Jones would have been proud to design.

OUT				IN			
hole		par	yds.	hole		par	yds.
1	bon voyage	4	419	10	the midway	4	429
2	the dell	3	205	11	ben nevis	4	373
3	the summit	4	374	12	ben lomond	3	151
4	heart of midlothian	4	391	13	the alps	5	521
5	the gate	4	407	14	easy street	4	316
6	high ball	4	433	15	paresis	3	179
7	long lane	5	534	16	the moat	5	518
8	brookside	3	214	17	teaser	4	427
9	the growler	4	439	18	home	4	319
		35	3416			36	3233

THE HISTORY

Charles "Chick" Evans's record in the 1916 U.S. Open at Minikahda Club may be the most unusual record in golf. Evans became the first golfer to win the U.S. Open with a 72-hole score under 290. His record-setting 286 stood for 10 years, until Tony Manero shot 282 to win the 1926 Open at Baltusrol. So far, no other U.S. Open 72-hole record has lasted as long. Evans set a second record that year—he won the U.S. Amateur at Merion to become the first golfer to win the U.S. Open and U.S. Amateur in the same year. Bobby Jones is the only golfer to have ever matched that feat; he did it in 1930, the year he won the Grand Slam.

Perhaps what is most remarkable about Evans's record at Minikahda is that he set it playing with only seven clubs. In that era, golfers could carry as many as they wanted. But Evans felt that all he needed was a 2-wood, 3-wood, 2-iron, 4-iron, 7-iron, 9-iron, and putter. He had a smooth, rhythmic swing and could control the ball with any club. Because his weakness was putting, he would sometimes take as many as four putters out on the course. He only used one putter at Minikahda.

Evans, the son of a Chicago librarian, took up golf as a caddie at Edgewater Golf Club. When he turned 16 in 1906, he started playing golf because of USGA rules, which barred caddies from playing as amateurs after age 15. Surprisingly, the 1916 Open was Evans's first national championship. He was often in contention in the Amateur but would always lose in the semifinal matches. He made the finals once in 1912, where he lost to Jerry Travers. Evans won the 1911 French Amateur and eventually won nine Western Amateurs as well as the 1920 U.S. Amateur. He played in tourna-

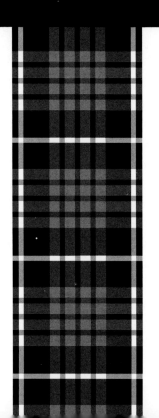

MINIKAHDA CLUB

•

Minneapolis, Minnesota

•

6,640 yards, par 73

•

Designed by Robert Foulis and William Watson

•

Redesigned by Donald Ross and Ralph Plummer

Chick Evans played in tournaments until he was 71 years old.

ments up to age 71, when he played in the 1961 U.S. Amateur at Pebble Beach. Evans died in 1979 after a fulfilling life of golf.

The 1916 Open, with 95 entries, was the last to field fewer than 100 players. There were 141 on the roster the year before at Baltusrol and 165 in the famous 1913 Open at The Country Club of Brookline. Although small, the 1916 Open was host to some of the greatest golfers in the world, including Walter Hagen, Francis Ouimet, Jim Barnes, Jock Hutchison, and defending champion Jerry Travers. In preparation for the Open, Evans brought his caddie up to Minneapolis and picked out a new putter. A heavy rainstorm soaked the course just before the start of the Open, making it softer than normal and a little easier, thanks to slower greens. In the first round of the 36-hole opening day, Evans shot a 32 on the front nine. He popped up to a back-nine 38, but the 70 was good enough to tie Wilfred Reid for the lead. That afternoon Evans took a three-stroke lead over Reid by shooting a 69.

The rain had stopped by the second day, and it was hot. Reid started with a magnificent front-nine 32, but faltered on the back nine, posting three consecutive sevens to wind up with a 43 and drop out of contention. Evans shot a third-round 74; not bad, but not good enough to secure the title. Hutchison shot a third-round 72, and then closed with a final-round 68 to shoot 288 and become the first golfer to break 290 in the U.S. Open. Barnes followed with a 289 to become the second 290 breaker. Surprisingly, the 288 wasn't good enough to win. Evans was on a mission. He wanted to birdie the 525-yard, par-5 13th hole. A creek cut across the fairway about 100 yards short of the green. Going for the green was a gamble, but Evans did it successfully with a solid drive followed by a brassie second shot. He sewed up the hole with a two-putt for birdie. He hit the short par-4 18th in regulation but three-putted for a bogey and final-round 73 to finish with a 286. Although he wasn't the first to break 290, his Open record lasted 20 years.

Evans went on to win the Amateur. The next year the United States entered World War I, so he remained the double national champion for three years.

THE COURSE

Even though Minikahda Club is only 6,640 yards and a par 73, it can be a tough course because of the natural Minnesota terrain. Thousands of trees are scattered over the course, and small hills sit in the middle of fairways. Minikahda has what is often considered the easiest hole in the upper Midwest. The 475-yard, par-5 14th is a straight hole with a reasonably wide fairway. Even a mid-handicap golfer can hit the green in two and putt for an eagle. It helps in recovering from all-too common disasters on the 10th hole, a 436-yard par 4 with a green sitting atop a large mound. The green is virtually impossible to hit in regulation, especially if the tee shot can't reach the green. The 10th hole runs parallel to the 432-yard, par-4 2nd, which resembles 10 but can be even more dangerous. Excelsior Boulevard runs down the right side of the fairway, and many tee shots can be seen cruising down it.

Those holes can create problems, but the two par 3s are even more troublesome. The 190-yard, par-3 6th hole boasts the only water hazard on the course. A pond that runs down the left side of the fairway and up to the left of the green has swallowed many a golf ball. Still, it is possible to get down in two for a bogey if a tee shot splashes down. Water does not plague the 160-yard, par-3 4th hole. Instead, the green rests on top of a steep mound heavily guarded by bunkers and trees. A tee

shot that veers right hits the mound and kicks down to France Avenue. Other tee shots bounce to the front or left of the green. The pitch shot is blind, and, if it's the third shot off the tee after an out-of-bounds shot, a six is about as good as a golfer can hope for. There is a possibility that 14 will be converted to a par 4, reducing par to 72. If that happens, there are not many recovery holes left. Minikahda has many holes that are just as tough in the 1990s as they were in the 1890s.

If you slice or hook your tee shot on this par 3, your ball will kick away from the green.

Chick Evans's U.S. Open record is even more impressive considering all the water and trees he encountered.

MYOPIA HUNT CLUB

•

South Hamilton, Massachusetts

•

6,440 yards, par 72

•

Designed by Herbert Leeds

•

Redesigned by Geoffrey Cornish

A U.S. Open victory is usually the crowning achievement of a golfer's career. Winning a second or a third is a rare feat, but winning four is extraordinary. Only four golfers have been four-time Open champions—Willie Anderson, Bobby Jones, Ben Hogan, and Jack Nicklaus. Each golfer was the best of his era.

Anderson was the first to claim four career Opens. He won his first in 1901 at Myopia Hunt Club in South Hamilton, Massachusetts. His next three Open wins came in an even more remarkable manner than Jones, Hogan, and Nicklaus. Anderson didn't defend his title in 1902 but returned in 1903 and won the next three Opens to become the only "threepeat" Open champion in USGA history. Unlike Jones, Hogan, and Nicklaus, Anderson could never fully savor his achievement. He died an alcoholic in 1910 at age 32—at the time, his death was blamed on arteriosclerosis. Anderson was the best golfer in America in the first decade of this century but was never able to fully enjoy the acclaim he earned.

Like all champions of the first 16 U.S. Opens, Anderson was a native of the United Kingdom and had immigrated to the United States to make money. He arrived in 1895 at age 17 with his father, the greenskeeper at North Berwick Golf Club in Scotland. Already a talented golfer, Anderson finished second in the 1897 Open. The next year he finished third in the Open, which was played for the first time at Myopia Hunt Club. Fred Herd won by seven shots over Scotsman Alex Smith. Anderson was the best Open player before World War I, finishing 11 times in the top 10, including his four victories.

His 1901 victory at the Myopia Hunt Club came in the first playoff in Open history and was the highest 72-hole winning score. Myopia proved so arduous that no player broke 80. Anderson shot 84-83-83-81—331, and Alex Smith shot a final-round 80 to tie Anderson. The playoff wasn't much different. Anderson shot an 85 to defeat Smith by one stroke.

The scores were high in part because gutta percha balls were still in use. The next year, the Haskell rubber-wound balls were introduced, increasing tee shots by about 20 yards. Anderson had a little trouble getting used to the new ball, and, although he did break 80 twice at Garden City Golf Club in Garden City, New York, he finished 11 strokes behind Laurence Auchterlonie.

In 1903, he set a U.S. Open record of 73 at Baltusrol but was tied again in the final round. Anderson shot an 82, allowing David Brown to catch him with a 76. In the playoff, Anderson shot another 82 but walked away with a two-stroke win. He successfully defended his title in 1904 at Glen View Golf Club in Illinois, breaking 80 in all four rounds and setting a tournament record of 303. His final-round 72 broke his own record set the year before.

Anderson returned to Myopia in 1905 to capture his third consecutive win and become the first career four-time U.S. Open winner. Again, it was Anderson and Smith dueling it out at Myopia. Smith, who was a stroke ahead of Anderson after the third round, shot a final-round 80. Anderson shot a final-round 77 to win by two strokes.

Anderson never won the U.S. Open again. He finished fourth when the Open returned to Myopia in 1908. But he never broke 80 in four rounds, leaving him eight shots behind playoff contenders Fred McLeod and Willie Smith.

Willie Anderson is the only golfer to win three consecutive U.S. Opens, in 1903, 1904, and 1905.

McLeod shot a 77 to win by six shots. Anderson did break 80 in all four rounds of the 1909 Open at Englewood Golf Club in New Jersey but only tied for fifth. The next year he played in three 36-hole matches in one week and died unexpectedly. Had he not died so young, he may have won another Open.

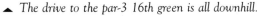
▲ *The drive to the par-3 16th green is all downhill.*

◀ *The difficult greens at Myopia Hunt Club make putting the key to any good round of golf.*

THE COURSE

Anybody who plays Myopia Hunt Club needs to do well on the first two holes because the next three can make life miserable. The major obstacles are the slick and undulating greens. The 1st hole is a short 274-yard par 4. Most golfers just have a flip wedge to the green, but the green slopes down to the left, and the flip wedge can easily bounce off. The next hole is a 487-yard, par-5 birdie hole. Golfers need to be even par or lower when they step up to the 3rd tee. The hole, 253 yards into the wind, is possibly the most difficult par 3 in New England. A fairway bunker in front of the green requires a 220-yard carry and the green is elevated. Many shots that carry the bunker kick off the green, making bogey 4 a good score. Bogey is also a respectable score on the 392-yard, par-4 4th hole, which doglegs left and down a hill. Its green is the most difficult on the course. In the 1905 Open, one player actually nine-putted the 4th green, which is slick and downhill, by stroking the putt too hard. His ball rolled off the green and into a water hazard. A deep bunker has replaced the water hazard, so it is now possible to putt into a bunker.

The shortest par 4 is the 260-yard 6th hole—not a birdie hole. Golfers need to lay-up short of a creek with a 6-iron and then pitch onto an elevated green. It's possible to drive close to the green, but a hungry pond down the right side of the fairway will catch pushes and slices to set up a double bogey.

The back nine has seven par 4s, one par 5, and one par 3. The par-5 15th hole is reasonable, and the par-3 16th is unusual. It is not as tough as the 3rd, but it is a bogey hole. The tee shot heads straight downhill toward the green, which is encircled by bunkers and guarded by knee-high rough that can swallow a poor tee shot. The 349-yard, par-4 13th is another hilly challenge. The tee shot is a lay-up short of a hill. At the top of the hill, about 70 feet above

If you hook or slice at Myopia, searching for your ball will be a futile effort.

the fairway, is the green. Golfers can see only the top of the pin on the approach, making the green easy to miss. The final two holes, set away from the rest of the course, are standard, parable par 4s. The only sensible strategy at Myopia Hunt Club is to do well on the first two and last two holes and survive the middle 14.

NATIONAL GOLF LINKS

•

Southampton, New York

•

6,745 yards, par 73

•

Designed by
Charles Blair MacDonald

When golf was first beginning in the United States, amateurs were considered the most important part of the game. Even though there were many pros, the United States Golf Association focused its attention on providing tournaments for amateurs like Bobby Jones and Francis Ouimet. Because golf had its beginnings in the United Kingdom, the USGA wanted to stir interest in tournament golf on both sides of the Atlantic Ocean. Interest in golf waned in England after the war broke out in 1914; when the United States joined the war in 1916, the game's popularity declined here as well. After World War I, there was a heightened interest in creating matches between British and American players. Top American amateurs would travel to Britain to play in the British Open and Amateur, and top British amateurs would cross the Atlantic to play in the U.S. Amateur and Open.

With the booming interest in international golf, the USGA felt it was time to conduct a match between American and British amateurs. In the spring of 1920, the executive committee of the USGA sailed to Scotland to meet with the rules committee of the Royal and Ancient Golf Club of St. Andrews to standardize the rules of the game. USGA committee members had the opportunity to play the Old Course at St. Andrews and other famous Scottish courses. One of these committee members was George Herbert Walker—grandfather of President George Herbert Walker Bush. Walker was a member of the National Golf Links of America and president of the USGA. He was a low-handicap player who liked the idea of American amateur golfers competing in Scotland.

When the executive committee returned home, they discussed the possibility of starting an amateur team match between the U.S. and Great Britain. Walker set up a committee meeting at the Links Club in Manhattan on December 21, 1920. On that day, he presented a plan for an international match and offered to donate an International Challenge Trophy. The next year an informal match was played at Hoylake, just before the British Amateur. The U.S. team defeated the British team 9 to 3 in the one-day match. The Americans did not play well in the British Amateur, but the victory over the British in the informal one-day match was some consolation.

In the spring of 1922, the Royal and Ancient Golf Club of St. Andrews agreed to send a team of top British amateurs to the U.S. in August to compete in the first Walker Cup, named after the man who inspired the event and donated the trophy. Walker's term as USGA president was over, and Howard F. Whitney, the new president, decided to hold the match at Walker's home club, the National Golf Links. The course was one of the best in the country at the time and was not too far from the USGA headquarters in Manhattan. The match was set up for foursomes the first day and singles the second day.

Whitney appointed 1910 U.S. Amateur champion William C. Fownes Jr. team captain. Team members included Chick Evans, Bobby Jones, Francis Ouimet, Jess Sweetser, Max Marston, Robert Gardner, and U.S. Amateur champion Jesse Guilford. Robert Harris was the British team captain, and his team members were Cyril Tolley, Roger Wethered, Colin Aylmer, C.V.L. Hooman, W.B. Torrance, John Caven, and Willis Mackenzie. British Amateur champion Ernest Holderness was unable to participate in the Walker Cup, because he didn't have time to travel to New York.

The original clubhouse, built in 1912, still stands, preserving the club's history.

▲ *Located between the 2nd and 16th holes, this was a true working windmill when it was built shortly after the club opened.*

◀ *Charles Blair MacDonald designed the course in the tradition of authentic links courses, in which the layout goes out and back from 1 to 18.*

Famous London golf writer Bernard Darwin came to the U.S. to cover the Walker Cup for the *London Times*. Darwin was a good golfer, and, when Harris became too ill to play, he appointed Darwin to take his place as team captain. Darwin and Tolley defeated Ouimet and Guilford in a best-ball match, but the Americans took the others. The next day Darwin played Fownes and was 3-down after the first three holes. Darwin played well on in and won the match 3 and 1 on the 17th green. Hooman defeated Sweetser on the first extra hole. That turned out to be the only extra-hole match in Walker Cup history. Points were not awarded for ties. The U.S. players came back to win, capturing the Walker Cup 8 to 4. After the Walker Cup, the group went up to the Country Club of Brookline to play in the U.S. Amateur. The British players didn't fare well; Sweetser won the tournament. Two years later the Walker Cup moved to St. Andrews, where the U.S. won again. The Walker Cup proved to be enormously popular and increased interest in golf around the world. The United States consistently does well in the matches, with 29 wins to their credit.

THE COURSE

One reason the USGA selected the National Golf Links to host the Walker Cup was that it was the only genuine links course in the United States at that time. Another reason was the fact that many of the holes resembled some of the best holes in Scotland. Charles Blair MacDonald learned to play golf while attending school in Scotland. When he returned to the U.S., he designed the National Golf Links to represent a true Scottish golf course. The course goes out and back from the 1st hole to the 18th; this layout is in keeping with the traditional Scottish links design.

The 196-yard 4th hole, a par 3, is an exact duplicate of the famous Redan hole in North Berwick, Scotland. The tee shot must carry over a long, narrow bunker to an elongated green that falls off diagonally to the left. Four additional bunkers surround the green, so the odds are high that an approach shot will land in the sand.

The 478-yard, par-5 7th hole is an imitation of the Road Hole at St. Andrews, minus out of bounds to the right. Another St. Andrews replica is the 170-yard, par-3 13th, which is exactly like the 11th on the Old Course except that the tee shot must carry over water. MacDonald's American hole is the 359-yard, par-4 14th. The tee shot must carry back over the same water that cuts across the 13th hole. A successful tee shot still leaves a tight second shot to a round green that is surrounded by eight bunkers and a water hazard. Water hazards distinguish the National Golf Links from Scottish links courses, most of which don't have water. National Golf Links has eight water hazards over six holes. Still, golfers who play the National Golf Links enjoy the experience of Scottish golf.

National Golf Links was the first links course in the United States.

NEWPORT COUNTRY CLUB

•

Newport, Rhode Island

•

6,658 yards, par 70

•

Designed by W.F. Davis

•

Redesigned by
A.W. Tillinghast

THE HISTORY

When the United States Golf Association was founded in 1894 by members of St. Andrews, Shinnecock Hills, The Country Club at Brookline, Chicago Golf Club, and Newport Country Club, the new USGA executives made organizing national championships their first priority. Shortly before the USGA was formed, St. Andrews and Newport both conducted invitational tournaments for amateurs. Newport staged a stroke-play event, and St. Andrews held a match-play tournament. Both declared their winners national champions, a controversy that ultimately convinced the clubs to form the USGA.

Theodore A. Havemeyer, the first USGA president, donated a $1,000 trophy for the national amateur championship that the USGA planned to conduct at Newport in September 1895. Because there were so many golf professionals in the U.S. that had emigrated from the United Kingdom, the USGA also decided to conduct an Open championship in which pros and amateurs could compete. The Open was to be secondary to the national amateur tournament. The Amateur was more important because amateur golfers were considered to be superior to golf pros, who worked for a living.

The USGA had to move the tournaments back to early October because the city of Newport was also hosting the America's Cup that year. Golf was so new in 1895, the USGA feared that no one would be interested in going to a golf tournament when the America's Cup was taking place. Newport was just a 9-hole course back then. The Amateur was conducted as a match-play tournament and the pros and amateurs played four times around the Newport nine in one day. Charles Blair MacDonald, the

HOLE		YDS	HCP			PAR			HOLE		YDS	HCP				PAR		
1	THE FIRST	459	1			4			10	QUARRY	535	8				5		
2	THE COP	390	7			4			11	HARBOUR	298	18				4		
3	OCEAN	328	17			4			12	VALLEY	435	4				4		
4	GRAVES POINT	225	11			3			13	CLUB	151	16				3		
5	POLO SHED	451	3			4			14	PLATEAU	205	10				3		
6	LOOKOUT	383	13			4			15	BRENTON REEF	436	2				4		
7	LONG MEADOW	552	9			5			16	ISLAND	359	12				4		
8	WILLOWS	194	15			3			17	POND	441	6				4		
9	ORCHARD	432	5			4			18	HOME	384	14				4		
	TOTAL OUT	3414				35				TOTAL IN	3244					35		
										TOTAL OUT	3414					35		
										TOTAL	6658					70		
										HCP								
										NET								

Horace Rawlins won the first U.S. Open in September 1895.

hot-headed Chicago golfer whose complaints spurred the formation of the USGA, won the first National Amateur. He defeated Charles Sands 12 and 11 in the 36-hole final to take the Havemeyer Trophy home to Chicago.

As the amateur champion, MacDonald didn't feel the Open was worth playing. There were ten pros, all from the United Kingdom, and one amateur, from Canada, in the field of the first U.S. Open. Willie Dunn, designer of Shinnecock Hills and winner of the match-play tournament at St. Andrews, was the favorite to win the Open. Little attention was paid to Newport's new assistant pro, 19-year-old Horace Rawlins, who had just immigrated to the United States from Britain that January. Rawlins shot a 45 on the first nine and was four strokes behind Willie Campbell, the pro at Brookline, on the turn; Dunn shot a 43 for second place. On the second nine, Campbell shot up to a 49 and finished sixth. Rawlins shot a 46 to stay two strokes behind Dunn, who also shot a 46; James Foulis of Chicago shot a 43. The highest score in U.S. Open history was recorded by William Norton of Lakewood Country Club. He started with a 51-58—109 and then withdrew in frustration.

Rawlins's talent kicked in, and he shot back-to-back 41s for a 173. Dunn scored 44-42—175 to finish second. Foulis's final-nine 43 tied him with Canadian amateur A.W. Smith for third. Rawlins won $150, which was more than he earned in a year at Newport, for winning the Open but was not awarded a trophy. The USGA felt that, because pros were employees of private clubs, the trophy should be awarded to the club instead of the pro. Dunn

▸ *The wind and the bunkers are the deciding factors of a low score.*

➥ *Climbing the hill to the clubhouse is a relaxing end to a day of golf at Newport.*

The wind off the ocean adds another challenge for players at Newport.

received $100 for second place, and Foulis was awarded $50 for third.

The next month the USGA staged a National Women's Amateur at Meadow Brook Club in Hempstead, New York. With the success of three national tournaments under its belt, the USGA was on its way to establishing national golf championships in the United States.

THE COURSE

Newport Country Club resembles a links course because of its oceanside location on the Atlantic. Wind can be a major factor in the progression of a round. It makes the par-70, 6,658-yard course play long. Golfers are immediately made aware of the obstacles they will face on the 459-yard, par-4 1st hole, one of the six par 4s over 400 yards. Two of the reasons the 1st hole is rated the toughest on the course are that it plays into the wind and that it has a slightly elevated green. The feel of the links comes on the 328-yard, par-4 3rd hole, which plays down to the ocean. The 225-yard, par-3 4th also runs beside the ocean and is even more links-like with the wind crossing the hole from the left. There are more long holes on the front nine than the back, but the wind backs up many shots, such as on the 552-yard, par-5 7th hole. The 432-yard, par-4 9th hole is also downwind, but it goes up a hill toward the clubhouse.

The back nine is the site of the original U.S. Open 9-hole course, but none of those holes remain. The 151-yard, par-3 13th hole and 205-yard, par-3 14th cover the land where the par-4 9th hole lay in the 1890s. The original 5th hole cut across the land where the 1st, 15th, and 9th holes can now be found. Other parts of the back nine are on top of the original 6th, 7th, and 8th holes. A round wraps up on the location of the original 1st, 2nd, 3rd, and 4th holes. The major difference is that the 15th, 16th, 17th, and 18th holes run south to north instead of the original north to south layout. Even though the first U.S. Open course no longer exists, a round at Newport brings the same challenges—the Atlantic wind and treacherous bunkers—to today's golfers as it did to Horace Rawlins and Willie Dunn.

OAK HILL COUNTRY CLUB, EAST COURSE

•

Rochester, New York

•

6,902 yards, par 71

•

Designed by Donald Ross

•

Redesigned by
Robert Trent Jones and
George and Tom Fazio

It's not unusual for a golf superstar to begin his Tour career with a major championship win. Jack Nicklaus did it. Bobby Jones, Walter Hagen, Julius Boros, Gene Sarazen, and Lee Trevino all did it. The last time a superstar launched his career with a major championship victory was 1968 when Trevino won the U.S. Open on Oak Hill's East Course. (John Daly kicked off his career by winning the 1991 PGA, but whether or not he'll join the ranks of golf's greats still remains to be seen.) The Open win rocketed Trevino to superstardom, especially since his victory made him the first golfer to break 70 in all four U.S. Open rounds. This accomplishment wasn't paralleled until Lee Janzen did it to win the 1993 Open at Baltusrol.

Trevino shot 69-68-69-69—275 to tie the record Nicklaus set the previous year at Baltusrol. What is even more impressive about Trevino's win and the record it set is that, before the 1968 Open, the world of golf had never heard of Lee Trevino. To that point, his golf resume consisted of a reputation in the Marines as a good golfer, a 1965 Texas State Open win, and a sixth-place finish at Baltusrol. With so few golf credentials, no one really noticed Trevino—and they certainly never imagined he would win—but his Open victory enabled him to play in more PGA Tour events. He won a little money in 1967 and continued to play on the Tour. His sixth-place finish in 1967 exempted him from qualifying in 1968. Trevino's career progressed steadily that year, but he was not yet a winner. His second-place finishes in Houston and Atlanta gave him a confidence boost just before the Open in Rochester.

Trevino started the round well on the East Course, but he wasn't in the lead. Burt Yancey,

Oak Hill's clubhouse looks the same today as it did in the 1930s.

a four-time PGA Tour winner, led the pack all three days with Trevino close behind. Trevino was at 204 and Yancey at 205 when they were paired together in the final round. They started off with bogeys on the 1st hole, but Trevino started parring. Yancey hit a hook under a tree on the 3rd then followed with a great recovery shot only to miss a five-foot par putt. This made Trevino the U.S. Open leader for the first time in his career. Then Nicklaus crept into contention; when Trevino took over the lead on 5, Nicklaus was only three shots back.

Nicklaus and Yancey played well enough to keep the Open interesting, but they never really threatened Trevino. A 30-foot putt, the longest he ever sank in an Open, on the 193-yard, par-3 11th hole widened his lead to three strokes. He also birdied the 372-yard, par-4 12th by dropping an 18-foot putt. Back-to-back birdies put him one-under par (par is 70 at Oak Hill for the Open) and virtually guaranteed his victory. He hit poor tee shots on both the 17th

and 18th holes, having to chop out of the deep rough to save par. Yancey collapsed toward the end, and Nicklaus settled for second. Trevino's victory at Oak Hill set up a career that included 27 Tour victories and two British Opens.

Trevino's 1968 Open victory may be Oak Hill's most historic major, but it's not its only one. In 1980, Nicklaus won the PGA Championship at Oak Hill. He only won one other tournament that year, the Open at Baltusrol. It was the last multiple-victory year of his PGA Tour career. The first Open on Oak Hill's East Course was won by Dr. Cary Middlecoff, a former military dentist, in 1956. He won his second career Open by one stroke over Ben Hogan and Julius Boros. The USGA didn't return to Oak Hill until 1984 when it staged the U.S. Senior Open on the East Course. Miller Barber, the only three-time Senior Open champion, won by two strokes over Arnold Palmer. Curtis Strange won his second consecutive U.S. Open in 1989 on the East Course after

Curtis Strange proudly accepts the trophy for winning the 1989 U.S. Open, his second in a row.

third-round leader Tom Kite fell apart. Oak Hill has been the turning point of many professional careers.

THE COURSE

Oak Hill Country Club was founded in 1901 on land that is now occupied by the University of Rochester. In 1926, the club moved to its present location and hired Donald Ross to layout 36 holes. Ross took full advantage of the wooded western New York landscape. He laid the East Course out around Allen's Creek, using the trees to obscure the creek and make holes even tougher. The course was moderately remodeled by Robert Trent Jones for the 1956 Open.

Trevino's four under-70 rounds worried the membership that their course was too easy, so they hired George Fazio and his nephew, Tom, to increase its difficulty. The Fazios brought Allen Creek more into play, especially on the

5th and 6th holes. Nonetheless, Nicklaus won the 1980 PGA by one stroke less than Trevino did in 1968. Strange's 1989 winning score, however, was three strokes higher than Trevino's, proving that the East Course is challenging—it's just been mastered by some incredible players.

The course's hardest hole is the 440-yard, par-4 1st, which may be considered the most difficult starting hole in the country. There is out of bounds to the right, deep rough, a fairway bunker on the left, and Allen's Creek crossing the fairway 80 yards short of the green. The creek is only a hindrance for second shots out of the bunker or rough, not for good tee shots. With trees and bunkers surrounding the green, it is easy to get into trouble if an approach shot is off target. Ben Hogan double bogeyed the hole three times and bogeyed once to lose the 1956 Open by a stroke.

The Fazio change on 5 inspired the club to name the hole "Double Trouble." Allen's Creek is just in front of the green, so the 406-yard par 4 makes it easy for a golfer to mishit an approach and feed the ball to the mallards. The green is the smallest on the course and easy to miss even if you get over the water. Number 5 may be tough, but 4 is even tougher. The green is bent to the right around a grove of trees in front of Allen's Creek. Many approach shots from the right side of the fairway hit the trees and splash down. Allen's Creek continues to the 167-yard, par-3 6th hole, which is a complete Fazio hole—4 and 5 were renovations of Ross's design. The hole plays into the wind, and it is not uncommon for a golfer not to clear the creek. Even Arnold Palmer made a quadruple-bogey 7 on the 6th in the 1984 Senior Open.

The longest hole at Oak Hill is the 594-yard, par-5 13th. In addition to its length, it has the narrowest fairway on the course with Allen's Creek crossing it 300 yards off the back

tee. The tee and second shots both invite disaster. The next par 5 is the 458-yard 17th hole, which is played as a par 4 in the Open. It's a par 5 for the members because the tee shot has to go uphill and avoid the trees on the dogleg only 240 yards away. In 1956, Hogan missed a two-foot putt on 17 that cost him a tie with Middlecoff. The 440-yard, par-4 18th hole can also cost a player a round. It is another dogleg right, but the major hurdle is hitting the green, which sits atop a steep hill. It's hard to get up the hill, and many shots that do bounce off the most rolling, narrow green on the East Course. Playing a round on Oak Hill's East Course gives you new respect for Trevino's magnificent feat.

▶ *Hitting the green is a difficult task at Oak Hill because of the hilly fairways.*

▼ *Undulating greens make three-putts common at Oak Hill.*

OAKMONT COUNTRY CLUB

•

*Oakmont,
Pennsylvania*

•

6,921 yards, par 71

•

Designed by
Henry Clay Fownes

A long with Baltusrol's Lower Course, Oakmont is one of the USGA's favorite sites for the U.S. Open. It has witnessed many historic Open events, including Ben Hogan's "Year of the Hawk" victory in 1953 and Jack Nicklaus's 1962 win over Arnold Palmer in a playoff for his first U.S. Open win and first professional win. Both victories played important roles in the careers of these two golf greats.

The first U.S. Open staged at Oakmont was the last to claim a Scottish-born champion when Tommy Armour defeated Lighthorse Larry Cooper in a 1927 playoff. The course was so tough even Bobby Jones wasn't in contention. A 13-over-par 301 sent Armour and Cooper to a playoff. That was the last time the Open was won with a score over 300.

The second highest score to win the U.S. Open also came at Oakmont. In 1935, Sam Parks shot a 299 to become the first golfer to break 300 in the Open. Parks was a local who had played Oakmont before; he had experience putting on Fownes's slick greens. The unlikely victor surprised the golf world by capturing the U.S. Open title—not surprisingly, it was his only professional win. Another one-time U.S. Open champion claimed his victory at Oakmont four decades later, in 1973. Johnny Miller shot a final-round 63 to set a tournament record and defeat John Schlee by a stroke. His victory was not quite as surprising as Parks, because it came at the height of his career.

In addition to unexpected winners and predictable victors, Oakmont has also been the scene of U.S. Open upsets. Tom Watson arrived at the 1983 Open at Oakmont the defending champion and the favorite to win again, so his loss to Larry Nelson was a shocking upset.

Nelson actually started the tournament rather poorly. A severe thunderstorm postponed the final five holes until the next day, giving Nelson time to regroup. When they returned the next day, Nelson sunk a long birdie putt on 16 and Watson responded by bogeying 17. These last holes gave Nelson the lead he needed and dropped Watson from contention.

The 1953 U.S. Open is arguably the most historic at Oakmont. Ben Hogan's win that year gave him the status of the only professional golfer to win three major championships—that is, in the modern era of majors, which includes the U.S. Open, the British Open, the Masters, and the PGA. A few years earlier, in 1949, Hogan made an amazing recovery from a nearly fatal car accident. Even more amazing than his

▲ *The gallery heads home after a long day at the U.S. Open in 1935.*

▼ *Henry Clay Fownes, Oakmont's founder and designer, holds the pin for Bobby Jones in the 1927 U.S. Open.*

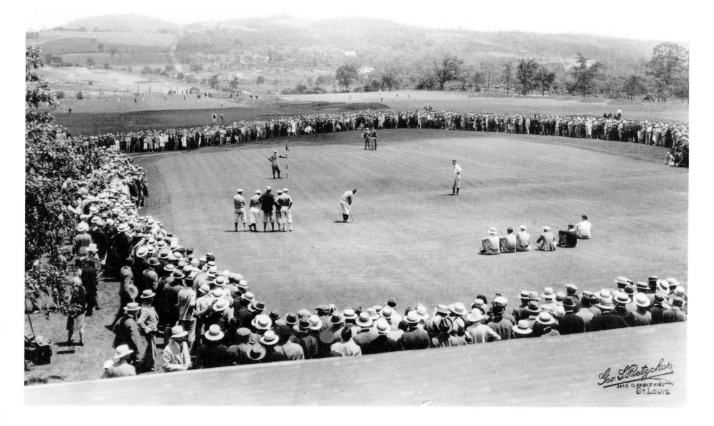

recovery was his successful comeback in professional golf. He won the 1950 and 1951 U.S. Opens but lost in 1952. Skeptics failed to recognize Hogan's determination and desire to win and predicted that his career had finally ended. His victory in 1953 proved them wrong.

Hogan had meticulous preparation habits. For example, before playing the Open at Oakmont he hit three balls off each tee—a draw, a fade, and a straight shot—to determine the best way to play each hole. This enabled him to develop the strategy he used throughout the tournament. It was obvious his technique was successful when shot a 67, the only score under 70, in the opening round. After scoring second-round 72, Hogan led the field by two strokes. On the 36-hole final day, Sam Snead shot a 73 in the third round to pull within one.

There was question as to whether or not Hogan's wreck-damaged legs could handle another 18 that day, and the odds were on the

smooth-swinging Snead to win his first U.S. Open. With three holes left to play, Hogan held his one-stroke lead. On those last three holes, Hogan shot three consecutive threes and erased all hope of Snead winning the 1953 Open. This victory came after Hogan's Masters win that year and before he captured the British Open (he didn't play in the PGA). No other pro, before or since, has won three majors in one year. That year became known as The Year of the Hawk in honor of Hogan, who was called The Hawk because of his killer instincts and intense concentration.

That was Hogan's fourth and last U.S. Open victory. Another great golfer who claims four Open wins is Jack Nicklaus. Nicklaus's first Open win came in 1962 at Oakmont—this was also his first professional victory. Even though he had just turned pro, he was already known as one of the great new golfers on the tour. As an amateur, he finished second in the 1960 Open at Cherry Hills and won the 1959 and 1961 U.S. Amateurs. The gallery at Oakmont in 1962 was largely made up of Arnie's Army, because Palmer was from Latrobe just 40 miles north of Oakmont. Palmer was the easy favorite that year due to his popularity, his success, and his experience. Besides the fact that he had played Oakmont over 200 times, he was the PGA Tour leading money winner and the 1962 Masters champion. An Open win would have put him on the road to the Grand Slam.

Nicklaus and Palmer were paired together in the first two rounds. Arnie's Army was vicious, cheering loudly for Palmer and calling Nicklaus "Fat Jack." Although Palmer was embarrassed by the army's attack on Nicklaus, he kept his

Arnold Palmer (left) congratulates Jack Nicklaus on winning his first pro tour victory at the 1962 U.S. Open at Oakmont.

The clubhouse, built in 1903, has hosted some of the greatest players in golf in its ninety years.

attention focused on the game. He led after the first two rounds and was tied by Bobby Nichols in the third. Nicklaus was two strokes back. Palmer bogeyed the 9th after hitting his tee shot into deep rough and shot a front-nine 35, the same as Nicklaus. The back nine was crucial. Palmer played a steady round but bogeyed 13 to finish with a 71; Nicklaus, on the other hand, birdied 11 and parred in for a 69. This tied them at 283 and sent them into a playoff round. (Nichols shot a final-round 73 and finished third.)

Ten thousand people showed up for the playoff, and almost all were members of Arnie's Army. Again, they cheered wildly for Palmer and ignored Nicklaus, especially when he hit a good shot. Palmer bogeyed the 1st hole, and Nicklaus birdied the 4th to take a two-stroke lead. After eight holes, Nicklaus led Palmer by four strokes. But on 9 Palmer did what he was known for and charged back into contention. He birdied 9 and scored back-to-back birdies on 11 and 12, narrowing Nicklaus's lead to one stroke. Arnie's Army marched forth in happiness until Palmer three-putted the 13th and dropped to two strokes back. On the critical

18th hole, Palmer bogeyed for a 74, and Nicklaus parred for a 71 to win the playoff. The Army may have been disappointed, but Nicklaus was thrilled to start off his professional career at Oakmont with his first U.S. Open and first professional win.

THE COURSE

Henry Clay Fownes founded Oakmont Country Club in 1903. He was confident that his golf knowledge and skills, he won the 1910 U.S. Amateur, would enable him to design a superb golf course. Fownes set out to design the most difficult course in the United States. The land that he purchased was divided by a railroad track; the Pennsylvania Turnpike was eventually built beside the tracks. Although the tracks could be considered an obstacle, they give Oakmont character because it lay on both sides of the gorge.

The two elements Fownes chose to concentrate on when planning Oakmont's difficult design were sand traps and testy greens. It is virtually impossible to play a round at Oakmont

*The Church Pew can bring an early death
to a player on the 3rd or 4th hole.*

without landing in at least one bunker, if not 18. There are 190 bunkers at Oakmont, including the infamous Church Pew. The Church Pew is a forty-by-sixty yard fairway bunker with seven grass ridges located between the 3rd and 4th holes. A tee shot in the Church Pew can cost two or three shots just to get back to the fairway.

Fownes's greens are reasonably large. This makes them easier to hit in regulation and easier to three-putt. They are slick and undulating, making even a two-foot par putt challenging. When Larry Nelson sunk that long putt on 16 in 1983, he accomplished a feat few golfers will match.

Nelson was lucky, because Oakmont's final four holes can ruin a scorecard. The 15th hole is 453-yard par 4 that includes all Fownes's challenges: four fairway bunkers, four greenside bunkers, and a slick putting surface. You may be lucky enough to keep your ball out of the sand only to find yourself three-putting on the long, narrow green. The par-4 17th is 322 yards and looks deceivingly like a birdie hole. There are eight bunkers lying in wait within 100 yards of the green. It takes a perfect tee shot to get close to the green followed by a perfect wedge to avoid kicking off the elevated green and into a bunker. The 18th hole won't help regain any lost strokes on the previous three holes; it's a 456-yard, uphill par 4. The green is difficult to reach in regulation because of the long, uphill, heavily bunkered layout, and double bogeys are common. Of course, this could be said of any hole at Oakmont. Fownes's design is just as difficult today as it was ninety years ago.

It takes a long hitter to reach the 18th green in regulation.

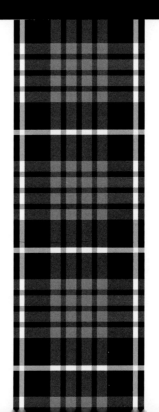

THE HISTORY

If you are a member of a country club where you play golf and enjoy all the other recreational facilities, you should be thankful that Olympia Fields Country Club, located in the south Chicago suburb it's named after, was formed in 1916. There were many country clubs in the United States before 1916, but most were created for outdoor recreations that did not include golf. Golf courses began appearing at clubs when the game's popularity increased in the 1890s. Many of the clubs formed at that time were dedicated only to golf, neglecting family recreation.

In 1913, Charles Beach, a Chicago businessman, recognized golf's immense popularity and the overcrowdedness of single 18-hole golf clubs. Beach set out to find a large amount of property near Chicago where he could develop the largest country club in the United States. He wanted four 18-hole courses and a spacious clubhouse where affluent Chicago residents could break away from life's stress for relaxing weekends—members could actually stay at the club all weekend and on vacations.

Beach took the Illinois Central Railroad down south of Chicago and spotted a 700-acre farm near the town of Flossmoor. Its rolling hills were crossed by a creek through an untouched forest. Beach knew this was the spot he'd been searching for. He called the club Olympia Fields Country Club because much of the recreation included Olympic events in addition to golf. Beach had no problem recruiting members, and the club's charter was signed on July 16, 1915. A small golf course was constructed in 1916 to get the club on its feet. The clubhouse was near the old farmhouse. The members could get to the club easily by taking the same train Beach took to find the land. Ac-

OLYMPIA FIELDS COUNTRY CLUB, NORTH COURSE

•

Olympia Fields, Illinois

•

6,857 yards, par 70

•

Designed by
Willie Park

The grandeur of the clubhouse at Olympia Fields set the standard for future country clubs.

tivity at the club slowed down during World War I. By the end of the war, there were two 18-hole courses and a large clubhouse. In 1921 a third course was opened; the next year the fourth was completed. The Fourth Course—now known as the North Course—was designed to serve as Olympia Fields's championship course. The club hired Scotsman Willie Park Jr., winner of the 1887 and 1889 British Opens, to design the course—his father, Willie Park Sr., won the first British Open in 1860. As a Scotsman experienced in golf, Willie Jr. entered the field of golf course architecture and opened an office in New York. His layout of Olympia Fields's new Fourth Course used all available trees, hills, and water. Unfortunately, Park died three years after the course was constructed; it turned out to be the last course he ever designed.

With 72 holes, Olympia Fields was the most well-thought out club in the United States and served as an example of country club develop-

ment based on golf and family recreation. The clubhouse resembled Windsor Castle, and there were 100 homes near the golf course, making Olympia Fields the first real estate-related country club. Olympia Fields Country Club was almost like its own city. The dining rooms could feed up to 1,400 members. The club added a hospital, fire department, and 2,000 caddies. Because of the club's prestige and excellent championship course, it has been chosen to host several major championships. Jock Hutchison won the Western Open in 1920, when it was considered a major, at Olympia Fields before the Fourth Course was open. Walter Hagen won the 1927 Western Open on the Fourth Course shortly after it opened. Olympia Fields was good to Hagen. In 1925, he won the second of his four consecutive PGA Championships at Olympia Fields by defeating "Wild" Bill Melhorn 6 and 5 in the 36-hole final match.

The second major championship at Olympia Fields was the 1928 U.S. Open. (The Western Open was played there in 1933, 1968, and 1971, but it was not considered a major once the Masters at Augusta National was started. Mac Smith won the 1933 Western Open, Jack Nicklaus won it in 1968, and Bruce Crampton won in 1971.) The U.S. Open at Olympia Fields was considered a downfall by Bobby Jones fans. Jones was the best golfer in the world, but he didn't seem to be taking the Open seriously in 1928. He was concentrating so hard on his Atlanta law practice that he didn't even bother to defend his 1927 British Open title. Jones played decently at Olympia Fields but not good enough to win. He exploded to a final-round 77, allowing Johnny Farrell to make up five strokes and tie him for the championship. They met in a 36-hole playoff, where Farrell shot a

first-round 70 to lead Jones by three shots. In the second round, Jones closed in with a 71 but that wasn't enough to beat Farrell's 73—143. Farrell's win was a victory for golf pros who were tired of losing to amateurs like Bobby Jones.

▶ *Hitting this par-3 green demands a long tee shot to get up the hill.*

▼ *Butterfield Creek winds through the course, testing the ability of even the most accomplished golfers.*

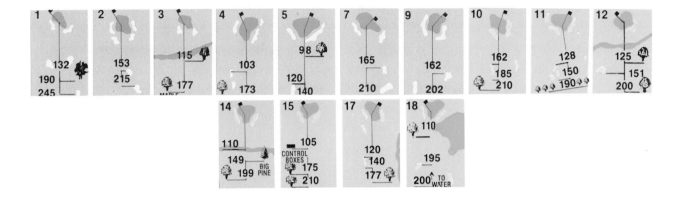

Olympia Fields changed dramatically after the Open. Two of the courses were closed and converted to real estate developments to help recoup some of the money lost during the Great Depression. The Fourth Course survived and was renamed the North Course; the South Course is a combination of the remaining parts of the First and Second Courses. Keeping the Fourth Course helped Olympia Fields attract another major championship—the 1961 PGA. Jerry Barber, an Illinois native, won his only career major out of his five Tour victories when he defeated Don January by a stroke in an 18-hole playoff. Olympia Fields set the standard for country clubs across the U.S.

THE COURSE

Members of Olympia Fields Country Club tend to prefer the North Course over the South. This is because golfers with a handicap above 18 find the South Course more difficult, largely due to Butterfield Creek swirling through 11 holes. The North Course is actually more difficult for low-handicap and professional golfers. This is because the creek comes more into play on good shots on the North Course but nabs bad shots on the South course. Butterfield Creek determines a golfer's fate on the 439-yard, par-4 3rd hole. The fairway drops down a 40-foot cliff, but it is possible to get over the cliff off the tee. The second shot has to clear the creek to reach the green. Approach shots often carry the creek only to bounce off elevated greens and into the water. Butterfield Creek zigzags across the wide fairway on the 444-yard, par-4 14th hole. Clearing the creek is easy with a solid tee shot, but slices and pushes will kick into the water. The second shot sets up a similar situation—a good shot will sail over a large bank behind the creek, but a poor shot will roll in the water. The shortest par 4 on the North Course is the 368-yard 5th hole. It looks like a birdie hole on the scorecard, but members often choose to lay-up before a wide bunker in front of the green. If you don't think you can carry the bunker with your second shot, you go for a pitch and a par putt.

One hole Butterfield Creek doesn't cross is the 455-yard, par-4 18th, a 495-yard par 5 from the white tees. A long pond sits to the right of the fairway along the last 150 yards toward the green. Whether you're playing it as a 4 or a 5, slices sleep with the fishes. Between the pond and the creek, water controls a round of golf at Olympia.

THE HISTORY

After the third U.S. Open at Olympic Club's Lake Course, people began to wonder if the hilly, tree-lined course was not some haunted place where golf's best see their careers end in major championships. The Open in 1987 saw little-known Scott Simpson snatch victory from the man who dominated professional golf in the late 1970s and early 1980s—Tom Watson. A sentimental favorite to win after struggling for three years, Watson approached the last hole grasping for a chance to tie Simpson only to see a dead-on chip shot roll to the edge of the cup and turn to the left.

And so Watson joined the ranks of Ben Hogan and Arnold Palmer, two other superstars who suffered fatal blows amidst the massive trees of Olympic. Thirty-two years earlier, in the 1955 Open, Hogan had nearly sealed a record-setting fifth Open title when Jack Fleck, a municipal course pro from Davenport, Iowa, birdied two of the final four holes to tie him. In the final round, Fleck was walking off the 10th tee when he heard cheering from the nearby 18th green. The gallery was cheering for Hogan, who had just finished with a 70—287. Hogan walked off the green, handed the ball to Joe Dey of the USGA, and said, "This is for Golf House." He thought he was donating a memento of the only five-time U.S. Open winner.

Fleck had to play the last eight holes one-under to catch Hogan. He was playing well until he bogeyed the 14th, then the fans stopped following him. "When I made bogey, I thought to myself, 'They think I'm all through,'" recalled Fleck. He proved them wrong by hitting his second tee shot on the

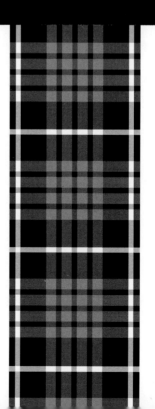

OLYMPIC CLUB, LAKE COURSE

•

San Francisco, California

•

6,808 yards, par 70

•

Designed by Wilfred Reid

•

Redesigned by Robert Trent Jones

par-3 15th eight feet from the hole and sinking the putt. The fans returned. He followed with pars on the tricky 16th and 17th holes. Hogan was in the locker room when he heard Fleck had to birdie 18 to tie him. "Good luck to him," Hogan said. And that's exactly what Felck got, luck. He lofted a half-7-iron about seven feet right of the pin. Facing a sensitive, sidehill putt, he calmly rolled in for a final-round 67 to tie Hogan.

The golf world was stunned. No one could believe that a club pro from Iowa had tied the best golfer in the world. Still, everyone assumed Hogan would kill Fleck, who would be intimidated, in the playoff. "I never felt that way. I felt I could always hit the ball tee to green well. If I could just do that, I could win," Fleck said.

◀ *Jack Fleck proudly accepted his 1955 U.S. Open Trophy.*

▼ *Billy Casper reads a green at the 1966 U.S. Open.*

And he did just that. He matched Hogan shot for shot. When the pair reached the 18th hole, Fleck was a stroke ahead of Hogan. Hogan still had a chance to catch Fleck, but Olympic wouldn't let him. His left foot slipped on some sandy turf, and he heeled his tee shot into the left rough. His lie was awful, and it took him two shots just to escape the rough. He holed an impressive 30-footer for double bogey, but Fleck's par gave him a three-shot victory. "I never wished anything bad on Hogan. When I saw him in the rough, I didn't think, 'Oh boy, this is wonderful.'"

Eleven years later, in 1966, Billy Casper upset Arnold Palmer when Palmer collapsed on the final nine while striving to break the tournament record. The two were paired together in the final round. Palmer roared out with a 32 on the front nine to take a seven stroke lead over Casper and the rest of the field. Palmer appeared to have secured the win at the turn. The problem arose because Palmer was convinced he had the Open won, and he started thinking about breaking Ben Hogan's 1948 tournament record of 276. All he needed was a 36. While Palmer concentrated on breaking the record, Casper tried to ensure a second-place finish. Palmer bogeyed the 10th and 13th holes and dropped his lead to five shots. The par-3 15th was the pivotal hole. Palmer bogeyed yet again and Casper birdied to cut the lead to three shots with three holes to go. That's when Palmer lost it. On the 16th, a grueling 604-yard par 5, he hooked his tee shot into the trees. That lead to another bogey answered by Casper with another birdie. It was no surprise when Palmer bogeyed 17, and Casper parred to tie him. Palmer's fate rested on the green where he made a difficult two-putt par. Casper also parred, setting up an 18-hole playoff the next day. The playoff was the fourth

Small, slick greens make two-putting an almost impossible task.

round all over again. A 33 on the front nine gave Palmer a two-stroke lead, but the back nine wouldn't let him win. Casper tied him with a birdie to bogey on 11. Palmer's ultimate downfall came on the final two holes, where he recorded a bogey and a triple bogey. Casper won the playoff by four shots, 69 to 73.

In all three cases, the Open loss was more than a tournament defeat. It brought about the demise of a player's career. Hogan never emerged as a factor in a major again, and Palmer's career never fully recovered. Watson managed to win a generous check at the season-ending Nabisco tournament, but he hasn't challenged in a major since. Fleck's career featured two more wins, but he never again contended in a major. Casper did have a superstar record, but he lacked the charisma to be placed among the elite. Simpson followed his Open win with his worst year as a pro, dropping to 106th on the money list. He could be destined to join Fleck as one of the Open's fluke winners, especially since he lost a playoff at Hazeltine National for the 1991 U.S. Open to Payne Stewart.

THE COURSE

Olympic's combination of 30,000 eucalyptus, pine, and cypress trees with its ice-slick greens makes it demanding for any golfer. When Robert Trent Jones redesigned the course for its first Open, he used the massive trees to create a horror show. He added to the nightmare by narrowing the fairways with eight-inch deep rough to create landing areas only 25- to 40-yards wide and tightening the greens, leaving slick specks surrounded by a maze of deep rough and bunkers.

One of the most arduous holes is the 480-yard, par-4 17th, a 522-yard par 5 for members. It's the hole Palmer bogeyed to allow Casper to catch him in 1966. Two killer holes are the short but deadly 343-yard, par-4 18th—the hole that offed Hogan in the 1955 playoff—and the 288-yard, par-4 7th. The par 3s are also troublesome with their easy-to-miss greens. Bogeys on

▶ *Robert Trent Jones used Olympic's trees to shape tight fairways and narrow greens.*

par 3s are common in the U.S. Open. So birdies can make up a few strokes, as Casper's did on 13.

Trent Jones's redesign of the Olympic Club Lake Course mysteriously produced a course that turns a superstar's game to jelly, while bringing the best out of journeymen. It may just be a quirk of history, but the home of the eerie last hurrah stands as one of America's most macabre historic courses.

Olympic Club is wooded with over 30,000 eucalyptus, pines, and cypresses.

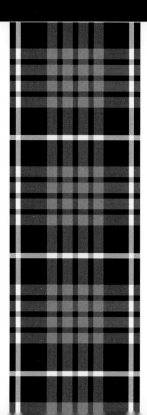

The Senior PGA Tour is the most successful new element in the world of sports. No other sport has the luxury of watching its past greats continue to display their skills while earning more money than they ever did during their heydays. If it wasn't for the Legends of Golf tournament held at Onion Creek Golf Club in Austin, Texas, the Senior PGA Tour might not have been formed. Prior to the formation of the Legends in 1978, there was a Senior PGA Championship. Unfortunately, it received little attention from golf fans, who viewed senior golfers as less talented.

That changed after the 1979 playoff between the best-ball teams of Roberto De Vicenzo and Julius Boros versus Art Wall and Tommy Bolt. The year before, when the first Legends of Golf was played, it was a simple television exhibition created by Jimmy Demaret, a three-time Masters champion from Texas who passed away in 1984, and Fred Raphael, the director of *Shell's Wonderful World of Golf*. Sam Snead and Gardner Dickinson won the uneventful tournament that year.

The 1979 playoff attracted fans to senior golf because of the extraordinary skill of the two teams. "That playoff showed a national television audience that senior professionals can play," Demaret said in 1982. Although De Vicenzo and Boros defeated Bolt and Wall in the playoff, both teams were birdie crazy. De Vicenzo and Boros went birdie crazy in the final round to force the playoff. They birdied the final three holes to tie Bolt and Wall. Once the playoff started, both teams birdied five consecutive holes. Most were the result of a great approach shot within 10 feet of the hole. The playoff came to an end on the sixth playoff hole, the 360-yard, par-4 16th. De Vicenzo hit

ONION CREEK GOLF CLUB

•

Austin, Texas

•

6,584 yards, par 70

•

Designed by Jimmy Demaret

Sam Snead and Don January won the
Legends in 1981.

his approach three feet from the cup; Bolt and Wall each hit the green but were more than 20 feet away. Both missed their putts, and Boros tapped in for victory.

The concept of watching golf legends play competitively attracted sponsors to future senior events and prompted the PGA to form the Senior PGA Tour division, creating an entire season of senior events parallel to events on the regular PGA Tour. The following year, Liberty Mutual became the title sponsor of the Legends of Golf, and three other events were sponsored by the PGA Tour. Within 10 years, the Senior PGA Tour grew to 41 events with a total season purse of $14,195,000. "I think the playoff had a lot to do with the start of the Senior PGA Tour because NBC was doing the telecast," said Bolt. "Making those birdies created a lot of interest in senior golf. You don't have to give it up just because you have a little age on you."

Golfers have to hit it long and straight to
carry the water on the par-3 11th hole.

THE COURSE

Although Onion Creek no longer hosts the Liberty Mutual Legends of Golf, it was the ideal course to give birth to the Senior PGA Tour. Demaret designed the course to be challenging for senior golfers of all abilities but not so overwhelming that it's not enjoyable. The course is only 6,075 yards from the white tees, so regular senior golfers can concentrate on hitting the ball straight and not worry about losing distance. It's a tight course, with Onion Creek winding its way across fairways and through thick trees. Onion Creek forms the outer circle of of the front nine, sitting to the right on holes 3 through 8 and traversing 11 and 12. It takes an awful mishit to land in the creek, but it's always waiting, just in case, to snare slices, shanks, and pushes. Straight shots up the fairway will take you to the green with one ball.

The 590-yard, par-5 18th is the signature hole because so many golfers have birdied it to win or tie for the championship. The green sits

atop a tree-lined hill, forcing Senior PGA Tour pros to hit two great shots to reach the green for an automatic birdie. But, if they push or pull the second shot, they're in trouble. The average golfer can lay-up short of the hill and pitch on for birdie or par. Onion Creek's contribution to the world of golf has ensured that today's golfers, such as Fred Couples, John Daly, Davis Love III, and Nick Price, will continue to entertain us in the next century.

▸ *Only a straight shot will get you through the tree-lined fairway on 12.*

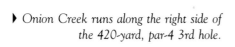
▴ *Golfers discuss the undulations of the 10th green.*

▸ *Onion Creek runs along the right side of the 420-yard, par-4 3rd hole.*

PALMETTO GOLF CLUB

•

Aiken, South Carolina

•

6,380 yards, par 71

•

Designed by Herbert Leeds

•

Redesigned by
Alister MacKenzie

During the Civil War, soldiers from the North were introduced to warm Southern winters. Once the war was over, veterans frequently escaped the harsh Northern winters by returning to the South to vacation. As golf became increasingly popular over the next few decades, Northerners found playing golf in the South an ideal winter activity. Palmetto Golf Club was founded in 1892 for this very reason.

In the 1890s, many wealthy New England residents escaped the snow by traveling to Aiken, South Carolina, to play polo and hunt. One of these wealthy New Englanders was Thomas Hitchcock, an avid sportsman from New York. Hitchcock first conceived of Palmetto when he built a 4-hole golf course so that he and his cronies could add the new game to their recreational choices. This course became popular quickly because of the beautiful landscape and the warm weather, convincing Hitchcock to expand the clubhouse and increase the course to 18 holes in 1897.

In 1900 Harry Vardon toured the United States with the Prince of Wales to promote the new Vardon Flyers. During his tour, Vardon was invited to play Palmetto. He was not, however, invited into the clubhouse because he was a golf professional. Exclusive golf clubs were common in that era. Only the wealthy could afford to play the game, and golf pros were considered blue-collar workers.

The success of Palmetto set the standard for golf vacation spots in the South. Even Augusta National resulted from its success. While designing Augusta National in 1932, Alister MacKenzie spent some time at Palmetto adding bunkers and elevated greens. There has always been a strong relationship between the two

clubs. In fact, several members of Palmetto assisted in forming Augusta National and organizing the Masters. Although the pros loved playing in the Masters, the purse was disappointingly low. Interest in the tournament waned, and during World War II the Masters wasn't played at all. At the time the 1945 Masters would have been held, Palmetto president Eugene Grace invited top golfers to play in the Devereux Milburn Pro-Am, named in honor of a past president, to raise money for the Red Cross.

These professionals included Byron Nelson, Sam Snead, Craig Wood, and Sam Byrd. The players were drawn by the opportunity to make some money and get a few rounds of golf in when they would have been playing the Masters—the free dinner didn't hurt either. Nelson, winner of the tournament, said, "The main thing was that we went wherever we could go play and play for an extra dollar. You did anything you could to pick up an extra 25 or 50 dollars. Palmetto is a fine golf course, and I enjoyed playing it."

The pros were eager to return to Palmetto the next year, even though the Masters had returned, because it was a great chance to make some extra money and the Tour was not as well organized back then. Most of the players were club pros from the Northeast and Midwest—Nelson was from Inverness—and the clubs weren't open yet in early April. This gave the pros an opportunity to play the Masters and the Devereux Milburn Pro-Am. By 1946, the field had increased from 4 to 40. Several reknowned golfers claim wins to this tournament: Jug McSpaden in 1947, George Fazio in 1948, Lawson Little in 1949, and Ben Hogan in 1952. When Hogan was seriously injured in a car wreck in 1949, Grace sent

Palmetto's clubhouse was designed by Stanford White in 1902.

The view of the 18th green was much different in the early 1900s.

Palmetto Golf Club was established in 1892. William C. Whitney and Thomas Hitchcock originally built four holes with sand greens, presently the 16th, 17th and 18th greens.

Herbert Leeds later laid out the remainder of the first nine holes. By 1895 Palmetto had become an 18-hole course. Leeds and James Mackerell, the clubs first pro, laid out the remainder of the course.

Club President Eugene Grace and Vice President Eddie Rogers present the Devereux Milburn Pro-Am trophy to Ben Hogan and Bobby Goodyear in 1952.

him a telegram saying that the club missed not having him in the field and wishing him a "rapid and complete recovery."

The pro-am ended in 1953 as the Tour became more organized and the Masters purse grew. Still, today's pros enjoy Palmetto as much as pros in the forties and fifties. Ben Crenshaw, 1984 Masters champion, likes traditional golf courses like Palmetto. "I've played it twice. I go over there occassionally just to relax in a nice, quiet place to release the tension. The membership is very nice."

THE COURSE

Just looking at Palmetto's scorecard leads a golfer to believe that the course is easy because it is only 6,380 yards from the back tees. But elevated greens and severe slopes make it play about 500 yards longer. "It is a great routing job," says Crenshaw, noting that the elevated greens add considerable length. The 417-yard, par-4 13th hole, named the "Cabin" after an old cabin to the left of the green, plays more like a 562-yard hole because it rolls up a steep hill. Cabin is difficult to reach in regulation. Chip shots often bounce off the elevated green and into a bunker.

Obviously Palmetto demands good shots at all times, but within 50 yards of the green and 20 feet from the pin accuracy becomes essential. Pitch shots are challenged by firm greens, and putts have to overcome undulations that cause sharp breaks and fast paces. So, a good round at Palmetto is based on a good short game.

Palmetto also features scattered trees and several new bunkers added by Rees Jones in the

1980s. Golfers have to play well to score well, no matter what their handicap is. Luckily, there are four sets of tees, allowing golfers of all levels to enjoy the challenging course. Nelson said, "What I like about it is that it is an accurate course." It defintely takes an accurate golfer to post a good score at Palmetto.

Elevated greens can make a hole 35% longer.

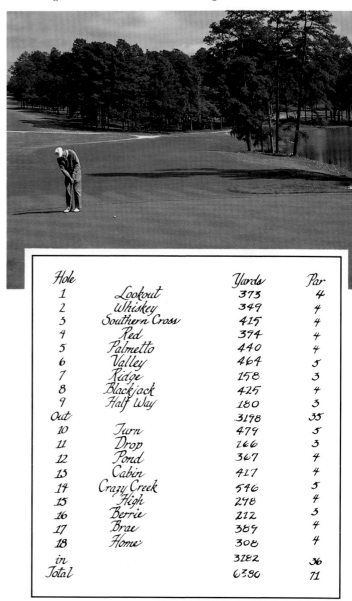

Hole		Yards	Par
1	Lookout	373	4
2	Whiskey	349	4
3	Southern Cross	415	4
4	Red	374	4
5	Palmetto	440	4
6	Valley	464	5
7	Ridge	158	3
8	Blackjack	425	4
9	Half Way	180	3
Out		3198	35
10	Turn	479	5
11	Drop	166	3
12	Pond	367	4
13	Cabin	417	4
14	Crazy Creek	546	5
15	High	298	4
16	Berrie	212	3
17	Brae	389	4
18	Home	308	4
in		3182	36
Total		6380	71

PEBBLE BEACH GOLF LINKS

•

Monterey Peninsula, California

•

6,806 yards, par 72

•

Designed by Jack Neville and Douglas Grant

•

Redesigned by Chandler Egan

THE HISTORY

Pebble Beach is the most famous golf course in the United States. It was the first true links course in the U.S. when it opened in 1919 and, over the years, has been the site of many important events. The USGA has conducted three U.S. Amateurs and three U.S. Opens at Pebble Beach in addition to the annual Bing Crosby National Pro-Am (now the AT&T Pebble Beach National Pro-Am). Pebble Beach has been home to the tournament since 1947 when Crosby moved it from Rancho Santa Fe Country Club in San Diego, starting the trend of celebrity sponsors for PGA Tour events. That trend was eventually replaced by the wealthier corporate sponsors, but the format of the Bing Crosby National Pro-Am has remained constant since 1937.

Crosby moved his tournament to Pebble Beach after World War II because interest had waned in San Diego. He was a member of Cypress Point and was interested in moving his tournament there because of the links style course. Ted Durein, the sports editor of the *Monterey Peninsula Herald,* convinced Crosby to include Pebble Beach in the tournament in addition to Cypress Point, which eventually fell off the tournament list. Pebble Beach, on the other hand, has continued to be the foundation of the pro-am because the final round is always held there.

Pebble Beach was founded in 1915 when a real estate developer named Samuel F.B. Morse purchased 5,300 acres of land along Carmel Bay on Monterey Peninsula. His idea was to build a resort and residential development—a common concept today but a novel one at the time. Morse decided to add a golf course to the resort in response to golf's fast-growing

In the mid-1920s, a gallery watches a golfer trying to sink a putt on 18.

popularity, especially among the wealthy. Morse wasn't a golfer, but he was a smart man. He contacted Jack Neville and Douglas Grant, former California State Amateur champions and the best golfers in the state, to assist him on the golf side. Neville and Grant laid out the course so that as many holes as possible ran along Carmel Bay. The 6,314 yard, par-74 course opened in 1919.

Once Morse began to understand golf, he felt that Pebble Beach needed to be redesigned, especially since he had just convinced the USGA to conduct its first national championship in California at Pebble Beach. Morse hired Chandler Egan, the winner of the 1905 and 1906 U.S. Amateurs, to make Pebble Beach a formidable par 72. Egan altered eight holes. His greatest change came on the famous 18th hole, now a 548-yard par 5 that runs along the

Sheep grazed on Pebble Beach land in 1919, the year it was founded.

A group of golfers tees off on the 6th.

rocky beach. Neville and Grant had designed it as a 379-yard par 4; Egan wanted to bring Carmel Bay more into play. He moved the tee back 169 yards to the left and placed it on a promontory. That forced golfers to hit away from the ocean or face big trouble.

The redesign of Pebble Beach brought it renewed attention. The USGA staged the 1929 U.S. Amateur there in the Bobby Jones era. Jones had won back-to-back Amateurs and was the defending champion. At one over par, he was the co-medalist with Eugene Homans in the 36-hole qualifying. Another one of the qualifiers was Johnny Goodman, an unknown player from Omaha, Nebraska. Goodman was so poor he got to California by jumping a cattle train. He shocked the world of golf in the first round by beating Jones 1-up. Despite Goodman's successful first round, he didn't go on to win the Amateur; it was won by Harrison Johnston in three extra holes against George Voigt. Goodman later proved his defeat of Jones wasn't a fluke when he won the 1937 U.S. Amateur, four years after winning the U.S. Open to become the last amateur to win the Open. Jones stayed in California for a few days after losing the amateur. He played Cypress Point, designed by Dr. Alister MacKenzie, and liked the course so much that he later hired MacKenzie to design Augusta National.

Two golfers who owe a debt to Pebble Beach are Jack Nicklaus and Tom Watson. Both won U.S. Opens at Pebble Beach but have other reasons to treasure the course as well. Nicklaus won his second career U.S. Amateur at Pebble Beach in 1961, defeating Dudley Wysong 8 and 6. That win inspired him to turn pro. "I fell in love with Pebble Beach," Nicklaus said. "The first time I saw it was my amateur days. If I could play only one golf course in the rest of my life it would be Pebble Beach." In his pro career, Nicklaus won three Bing Crosbys, one of them in 1972. Pebble Beach was good to him that year. After winning the Bing Crosby, he returned in June and won the U.S. Open. This was his third Open win, and it put him in contention to tie the record of four career U.S. Opens, which he did in 1980. Nicklaus's victory was a two-over-par 290, a high score created by the ocean wind. He beat Bruce Crampton by three shots, thanks to his famous 1-iron shot into the wind on the 209-yard, par-3 17th hole. The ball hit the pin and settled three inches from the cup.

Watson also had a great moment on 17 at Pebble Beach. In the 1982 U.S. Open, he was tied with Nicklaus when he pulled his tee shot left of the green and landed on the side of a mound. He was pin-high, but the pin was close to his ball, creating a tedious downhill chip shot. Watson lofted a soft sand wedge that rolled in for a birdie. He followed with a birdie on the 18th to win by two strokes. Winning the U.S. Open at Pebble Beach was a memorable

Pebble Beach's oceanside location makes it a true links course.

Many a golf ball has bounced off the rocks to a watery death on the 18th.

experience for Watson because it is his favorite course. He attended college at Stanford and played Pebble Beach frequently. "I used to play there like I was playing in the U.S. Open," Watson remembered. "I had dreams that here was Tom Watson against Jack Nicklaus in the last three holes. I had to par all three to win the U.S. Open. I never did. There were always a couple of bogeys." When Watson finished birdie-birdie to beat Nicklaus in the U.S. Open in 1982, his dream came true.

THE COURSE

Pebble Beach is the most serendipitous meeting of water and land in the world and provides the single most beautiful setting for a championship course. It is a true links course set next to the ocean. Its oceanside location makes it testy for two reasons. The first is the water itself. There are eight holes that run along Carmel Bay, so there are plenty of opportunities to send your golf ball to a watery grave. Powerful ocean winds are the other factor. It can be so hard at times that a pro playing the 107-yard, par-3 7th hole would have to hit a 3-iron to reach the green. The 7th sits on the tip of a small peninsula and is the second of five holes that run along the bay.

The scariest hole is the 431-yard, par-4 8th. It doglegs right over the ocean cliff. The tee shot has to settle near the edge of the cliff and the second shot must carry over the bay to a green next to the water. The last water hole is the par-5 18th. It's the hole everybody thinks of when picturing Pebble Beach. Many a golf ball has bounced off the rocks on 18. Golfers who try to stay away from the water can be blocked by a pair of trees on the right or they can land out of bounds. It is birdieable, but accurate shots are a must. This is true for any good round at Pebble Beach, unless the wind is wild.

PINEHURST RESORT & COUNTRY CLUB, NO. 2

•

*Pinehurst,
North Carolina*

•

7,020 yards, par 72

•

Designed by Donald Ross

onald Ross is often considered the most famous golf course architect in the country. Although North Carolina is definitely Donald Ross country, his courses can be found across the United States. Charles Blair MacDonald may have coined the term "golf architect," but Ross is the one who turned it into a profession. Like most golfers at the time, Ross was a Scottish emigrant born in Dornoch, Scotland, in 1872. He immigrated to the United States in 1898, where he dedicated his life to exposing Americans to his native sport. Ross was the first golf course architect to actually make a living at it. This status awarded him much prestige in the golfing world, and he quickly set the standards for his newly created profession.

Ross's talents were developed at an early age at Royal Dornoch Golf Club in the Highlands, which is still considered the northernmost world-class golf course in the world. His introduction to golf course design began when he was a teenager working as an apprentice for Tom Morris at St. Andrews. At age 21, he moved back to Dornoch and became the head pro and greenskeeper. During his tenure at Royal Dornoch, he redesigned the course, combining his own philosophy with the knowledge he had gained from Morris. Harvard Professor Robert Wilson admired the work he did at Dornoch and encouraged him to bring his expertise to the U.S. Ross accepted the proposal and moved to Boston in 1898, where he took a head pro job at Oakley Country Club in the Boston suburb Watertown. Scottish golfers were in great demand as club pros in the United States, so Ross knew he would make good money. Even though his primary motivation for moving to Boston was financial, his contribution to United States golf courses was more valuable.

The Tufts family of Medford, Massachusetts, wanted to develop a health resort in North Carolina. The idea was to create a winter resort in the South where New Englanders could go to escape the heavy snows. The Tufts originally hired Ross to be the winter pro at their new resort—he could return to Oakley in the summers. But, once they discovered he redesigned Royal Dornoch, they asked him to participate in the design of some of the five courses they planned to build on their sandy Pinehurst land. Ross eagerly agreed. He was reluctant to design sand greens, but the Tufts felt that they couldn't grow grass smooth enough to putt on. Sand greens were fairly common around the turn of the century because, at that time, there wasn't a method of pumping water onto a course.

The success of the Pinehurst course designs brought job offers from all over the country. Ross remains recognized as one of the most prolific golf architects in the U.S. Almost every state east of the Mississippi boasts at least one Donald Ross course, as do Missouri, Kansas, Minnesota, Iowa, Texas, Colorado, and California. Considering how difficult cross-country travel was in the early 1900s, Ross's courses cover an amazing territory.

In 1935, new grass-growing methods allowed grass to replace the sand. The New Englanders visiting Pinehurst felt lucky to be playing golf in the winter, but they couldn't get used to the sand greens. Ross, who was never satisfied with the sand greens, was happy to redesign them. He was enthused about incorporating his theory of approach shots producing birdies and good chips, pitches, and

Donald Ross, the course architect, hits the ball toward one of the sand greens he designed.

putts being necessary for par. The redesign made the Pinehurst course even more popular. This is especially true of No. 2, which was already well known despite the sand greens and has long been considered the true championship course.

The Tufts founded the North and South Amateur, staged at Pinehurst, in 1901; the North and South Open began shortly after in 1902. The tournaments were really geared toward northern golfers, but their popularity became more widespread soon after the grass greens were introduced. Many famous golfers are among the winners of the North and South

The clubhouse, which was built almost 80 years ago, has been expanded several times to accommodate the growth of the club.

Amateur: Francis Ouimet, Ed Furgol, Harvie Ward, Bill Campbell, Jack Nicklaus, Curtis Strange, Corey Pavin, Davis Love III, Hal Sutton, and Keith Clearwater. In the early years, Walter J. Travis won three times—1904, the same year he won the British amateur, 1910, and 1912. Jack Nicklaus, Jr. won the tournament in 1985 with his father in tow.

A more organized PGA Tour brought about the end North and South Open in 1951, but its list of winners is equally impressive. Ben Hogan won his first individual pro title at the Open in 1940; he won again in 1946. Other winners include Sam Snead (1941, 1950), Byron Nelson (1939), and Walter Hagen (1918, 1923, 1924). Surprisingly, Gene Sarazen and Tommy Armour both competed in, but never won, the North and South Open. But Armour, paired with Leo Diegal, did win the 1920 Pinehurst Fall Best Ball.

Pinehurst No. 2 dropped off the pro tour for decades after the loss of the North and South Open. However, the USGA conducted the

U.S. Amateur on the course in 1962. Labron Harris defeated Downing Gray 1-up to win the national title. The USGA returned to Pinehurst No. 2 in 1980 for the World Amateur Championship. The United States emerged from the field of 38 teams victorious by an impressive 27 strokes over South Africa. The pros finally returned to Pinehurst in 1973 for the outrageous 144-hole World Open, played over a two-week period. The $500,000 purse was the largest on the PGA Tour at the time. Miller Barber won the tournament by 6 shots over rookie Ben Crenshaw. The next year was tournament was shortened to 72 holes; Johnny Miller, who was having the greatest year of his career, won it. Jack Nicklaus won it in 1975 and Ray Floyd in 1976, and the list goes on with greats like Hale Irwin and Tom Watson. Pinehurst saw another pro tournament drought until 1991 when it staged the Tour Championship. Craig Stadler won that year, and Paul Azinger won in 1992. The tournament moved to California in 1993 while Pinehurst prepared for the 1994 Senior Open. The next pro tournament scheduled for Pinehurst No. 2 is the 1999 U.S. Open.

THE COURSE

P inehurst No. 2 is a trying course. Its difficulty is not easily attributed to the bunkers, the trees, the water, or the length. Instead, it is the clever combination of these challenges and their frustrating appearances in unexpected places around the course. Water doesn't even come into play for most players. The only water hazard is a pond in front of the 16th, a 531-yard par 5, but it is easy to carry on a tee shot.

The fairways are wide enough for good tee

▲ *The Golf Hall of Fame was once located behind the trees that enclose the 4th green.*

◀ *When Ross replaced the sand greens with grass greens in 1935, Pinehurst became a more popular site for tournaments.*

shots. But the tee shots have to land in just the right place so that approach shots avoid lurking bunkers. The only place length is a real difficulty is from the back tees on the par 4s. But most golfers don't have to worry about that. The single greatest challenge Ross presents to golfers playing his courses is the greens.

The number 4 green at Pinehurst used to put you near the World Golf Hall of Fame. Ross considered greens the source of a good score, so he designed them to be the most demanding part of his golf courses. Many of his greens were elevated with slopes off to the side. This forced off-line approach shots to dribble off the green, requiring a good pitch or chip to save par. The elegant fairways and greens of Pinehurst No. 2 represent the greatest course designed by the man who turned golf architecture into a profession.

PINE LAKES INTERNATIONAL COUNTRY CLUB

•

Myrtle Beach, South Carolina

•

6,609 yards, par 71

•

Designed by Robert White

Myrtle Beach, South Carolina, is the most popular golf vacation spot in the United States. Golf is the heart of Myrtle Beach; in fact, by the 21st century there will be over 100 courses along the Grand Strand. Originally, vacationers came to the area only in the summer to go to the beach. But, as golf began to increase in popularity, Pine Lakes International Country Club was built. This turned Myrtle Beach into a year-round vacation destination.

Pine Lakes was founded in 1927 and designed by Robert White, a native of St. Andrews, Scotland, and the first PGA president. The lake-spotted, 300-acre pine forest provided natural terrain that allowed White to design a tradionally challenging golf course. The quality of the course was superb, and the spacious clubhouse featured 62 rooms. The clubhouse was elegantly landscaped with brilliant azaleas and aromatic pine trees, making Pine Lakes the ideal setting for a relaxing vacation.

It wasn't until 1948 that another golf course, the Dunes Golf & Beach Club, was built in Myrtle Beach. Other courses soon followed in the wake of Pine Lakes's success, establishing Pine Lakes as the "granddaddy of Grand Strand golf." Pine Lakes was reorganized in 1944 by Fredrick Albert Warner Miles, the owner of several hotels in the South. His renovation of the clubhouse brought a resurgence of northern vacationers to the Myrtle Beach area, paving the way for the development of future golf clubs.

In June 1953, Henry Booth Luce and a group of sixty-seven Time, Inc. executives met at Pine Lakes to discuss forming a new sports magazine called *Sports Illustrated*. While there, they enjoyed relaxing in the clubhouse and playing the course. Perhaps this influenced the decision to include golf in the magazine's first issue on August 16, 1954. There were a few advertisements for golf products as well as an article titled "The Golden Age Is Now." The article noted that golf was the least popular participant sport in the country and ranked behind fishing, bowling, hunting, and boating. Another article, "Golf's Greatest Putt," describes Bobby Jones sinking a putt on the final green of the 1929 U.S. Open. This was the last article written by Grantland Rice, a founder of the Golf Writers Association of America, and was published posthumously. Rice died July 13, 1954. "I think this story by Grantland Rice is the perfect one with which to inaugurate our regular golf column," wrote Herbert Warren Wind in the article's introduction.

▲ In keeping with Scottish tradition, a kilt-clad starter sets up a group of golfers on the 1st tee.

▼ The hard-to-reach green on Pine Lakes' signature hole is guarded by a pond and three bunkers.

▼ When the clubhouse was renovated by Frederick Albert Warner Miles in 1944, vacationers traveled south to rediscover Myrtle Beach.

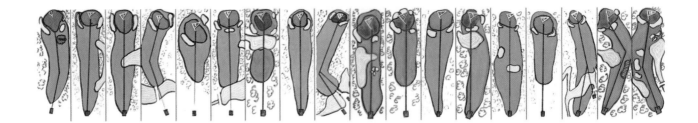

THE COURSE

In a 1980 fundraiser at Pine Lakes for the Tara Hall home for boys, Gene Sarazen shot a 78 at age 78. This is an impressive score on the traditional course with lakes and trees scattered everywhere. Every green is sandwiched by bunkers waiting to catch pushed and pulled shots, so a good shot has to be straight and have the proper distance to reach the green.

Pine Lakes's hazards make it play much longer than its 6,609 yards. Tee shots demand accuracy, because the fairways are walled with trees. There are also water hazards on 11 holes. The most difficult to avoid is the pond on the 159-yard, par-3 7th hole, the course's signature hole. The pond sits in front of the green and three sand traps surround it. A solid tee shot is the key to parring this hole.

Several strokes can be added to a scorecard on the last two holes. The 442-yard 17th, a par 4, doglegs left with a pond in the corner of the dogleg. Keeping the ball right avoids the water but extends the distance to the pin. The trees are thick around the green, and a sand trap in front of the green requires a full carry to land on the putting surface. The 18th hole, a 370-yard par 4, is a reflection of the entire course. It has two water hazards, eight sand traps, and more trees than anyone could count. Hitting the fairway is difficult because there is only a 50-yard wide landing area between fairway bunkers and a pond. Such difficult hazards are the nature of Pine Lakes.

Pine Lakes is only 6,609 yards from the back tees, but hazards, especially the eleven water hazards, compensate for the short length.

Target golf has become the standard style of golf course design. Golfers have to hit a target on the fairway, and then a target on the green to succeed in target golf. Missing the target means trouble. The basic concept of target golf is to reward good shots and penalize poor shots. Target golf wasn't popularized until the late 1970s, but its origin dates back to 1922 when Pine Valley Golf Club in southern New Jersey was finally completed after nine years of construction.

Today's Pine Valley is almost identical to 1922's. It is often considered the most difficult golf course in the United States because of its target design. Shots that miss the target may splash down or find their way into the trees, but most end up in a monstrous bunker. Pine Valley's difficulty brought it fame, and many golf course architects began incorporating the concept of target golf into their own designs.

Pine Valley was founded by George Crump, an enthusiastic golfer from Philadelphia. Crump, a member of Phildelphia Country Club, frequently traveled to Atlantic City with his golfing friends. On one trip, Crump spotted land that he believed would be perfect for a golf course. He purchased the 184-acre field in 1912 and formed a syndicate to develop the golf course. Crump received $1,000 donations from 150 golfers to help finance the course. The layout began in 1913 with the help of H.S. Colt, an English golf architect. Crump and Colt invented target golf by laying out all 18 holes separately. What they created resembles a 184-acre bunker with scattered tees, fairways, and greens. There were only two water hazards, so Crump and Colt spread them over four holes for additional target penalties.

PINE VALLEY GOLF CLUB

•

*Pine Valley,
New Jersey*

•

6,765 yards, par 70

•

**Designed by George Crump
and H.S. Colt**

The members of the 1936 Walker Cup Teams are shown separated by the trophy that the U.S. would win in the only shutout in Walker Cup history.

Crump died on January 24, 1918, while the course was still under construction. Unfortunately, he was never able to enjoy the acclaim Pine Valley received from the world of golf. Several of the holes were completed, however, before he passed away. Members got to play the course before it was officially finished in 1922, so that by the time it opened they had already spread the word about what a terrific course Pine Valley was. This convinced the USGA to conduct the 1936 Walker Cup match at Pine Valley, which the United States won over Great Britain and Ireland 9 to 0 for the only shutout in Walker Cup history. The gallery included over 3,000 golf fans, but the immense bunkers and thick trees didn't accommodate them well. For this reason, the club decided not to stage anymore tournaments.

In June 1960, Fred Raphael, the producer of *Shell's Wonderful World of Golf,* started the television series at Pine Valley in a match between Byron Nelson and Gene Littler. Raphael chose Pine Valley not only because it is a great golf course but also because it is close enough to New York City that the Filmways crew could easily get to the course. The match was an experiment to see if television was ready for a show intended to be a popular winter diversion for snowbound golfers. "They were learning and just getting started," Nelson remembered. "It was so horribly slow. It took two days to film 18 holes. It wasn't like I was playing a friendly round of golf. It was weird." Nelson and Littler each had to wait at least 30 minutes between shots while the cameras were being set up. "They had all sorts of problems," Nelson said. "They ran out of film, and the cameras made a lot of noise, so it was hard to even concentrate."

Nonetheless, the match between Nelson and Littler was a good one. Nelson teed off first and duck hooked his tee shot into the rough. The cameraman told him to take it over, but Nelson always abided by the Rules of Golf and played his ball where it landed. The awkward format made both players a bit nervous. "Normally Gene took the club back very smoothly and set it up at the top of his swing," Nelson said. "He was rushing that day and not getting the club set at the top of his swing." Nelson bogeyed the 1st hole, but his cool mind kept him going while the fast-swinging Littler was having problems. His swift backswing was causing him to miss the targets. On the treacherous 225-yard, par-3 5th hole, Littler blocked his tee shot into the woods on the right. He chili-

dipped the ball into a pot bunker and finished the hole with a quadruple-bogey 7. Because the match was stroke play instead of match play, Nelson's par on 5 secured his victory. He posted a three-over 38 on the front nine, and Littler struggled with a 42.

"We started as soon as it was daylight, and we only got in nine holes that day," Nelson recalled. "We were staying in the cottages at Pine Valley, and that evening Gene came up to me and said, 'Boy I played badly today,' and I said, 'Yeah, you didn't play like you normally do.' I knew his game because I had seen him play a lot." Nelson gave Littler a tip, telling him to slow down on his backswing. The two of them headed out to the practice range where Littler practiced Nelson's advice. Littler played well on the back nine, shooting a 34 for a 76; Nelson shot a 36 to post a 74 and win the match. If it had been match play, Littler would have won 1-up.

Narrow, well-guarded greens are the ultimate targets at Pine Valley.

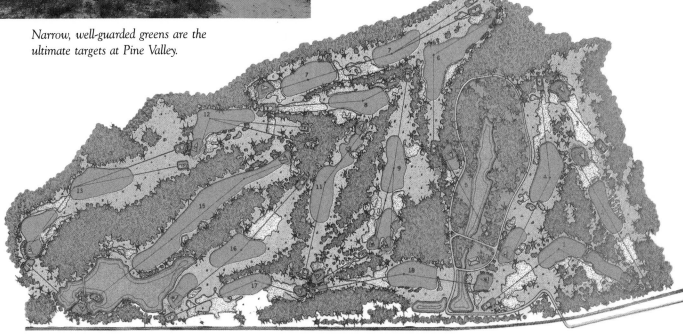

That match at Pine Valley may have been cumbersome for the players and the crew, but the learning process had started. "Later they were able to do the matches in one day," Nelson explained. The techniques Raphael and the Filmways crew learned at Pine Valley led to 92 matches aired over nine years. If the Nelson-Littler match hadn't been successful, *Shell's Wonderful World of Golf* might not have made it to television.

Sand traps, trees, and water hazards are essential elements of a target golf course.

THE COURSE

Target golf is especially difficult at Pine Valley. No hole is an automatic birdie, but several are automatic double bogeys. The target greens are the most difficult to hit. Because Pine Valley is located 200 feet above sea level, the highest spot in New Jersey, many of the greens are elevated and shots even slightly off line can sail down into a deep bun-

ker or thick trees. The green target is nearly impossible when the fairway target is missed.

The 585-yard, par-5 7th is the epitome of a target golf hole. The tee shot has to carry the sand on an island fairway; the second shot then has to carry the sand on another island fairway; the island green is also surrounded by sand. It's a target-to-target-to-target hole with thick trees on both sides. The 603-yard, par-5 15th hole is nothing but a giant target fairway. The tee shot has a reasonable carry over water, so hitting the fairway is possible. It's the second shot that kills golfers. The hole slopes sharply uphill and the fairway narrows dramatically, demanding a long, dead-straight shot to get within a reachable distance of the green. The steep uphill slope makes it unrealistic to reach in two, even if you're a heavy hitter like John Daly. Crump's and Colt's frightening concept is still setting the standard for golf architects 70 years later.

Missing the fairway target on a drive makes hitting the green target almost impossible.

Since 1948, the Riviera Country Club has been known as "Hogan's Alley." Ben Hogan hasn't strolled down that alley in a long time, but his spirit and memory live on at Riviera, the site of two historic moments in his career. In 1948, Hogan went to Riviera as the defending champion of the Los Angeles Open and successfully retained his title. That June the U.S. Open was played at Riviera; it was the first Open played in California. Hogan won the tournament, making it the second major championship of his career. The month before he won his first career major, the PGA Championship. The U.S. Open victory was a great asset to Hogan's career, considering he was 35 years old and hadn't won a major until that year.

With two consecutive L.A. Open victories at Riviera, Hogan was ripe to win his first U.S. Open on the same course. An opening-round 67 tied him for the lead with defending champion Lew Worsham. Hogan was harrassed by a pair of runaway dogs that kept barking at him from the gallery in the second round, causing him to slip to a one-over-par 72. Sam Snead took over the lead with a tournament-record 138. Snead's lead didn't last long. He played the final two rounds on Saturday three over par and opened the door for Hogan.

Hogan posted a third-round 68 and kicked off the final round with a birdie on the 501-yard, par-5 1st hole. Hogan played even par the rest of the way and stepped onto the 18th tee with a one-shot lead over Jimmy Demaret. The 18th hole is a difficult 447-yard par 4, and the potential for a bogey to force a playoff was strong. Hogan hit a long iron six feet from the hole and sunk the putt for a birdie and a final-

RIVIERA COUNTRY CLUB

•

Pacific Palisades, California

•

7,029 yards, par 71

•

Designed by George C. Thomas, Jr. and Billy Bell

round 69, setting a new U.S. Open record of 276.

Hogan's confidence was at an all-time high after winning two majors, and he went on to win eight more tournaments that year. The winning streak made him 1948's leading money winner and player of the year. He celebrated his great year by buying a Cadillac to drive around the country in 1949. He didn't defend his Los Angeles Open title in 1949 but did win the Bing Crosby and Long Beach Opens. He lost the Phoenix Open in a playoff against Demaret. On February 2, Hogan and his wife, Valerie, were driving back to his hometown of Fort Worth, Texas. They were traveling on a two-lane road near Van Horn, in west Texas, that was blanketed with fog when a Greyhound bus passed a slow truck in the oncoming lane.

Hundreds looked on as Ben Hogan teed off in the 1948 Los Angeles Open, which he won for the second year in a row.

A bird's-eye view of the action at the 1949 Los Angeles Open.

The bus hit the Cadillac head-on. Just before impact, Hogan threw himself over Valerie to protect her and that saved his life. The steering wheel slammed into the driver's seat, nicking Hogan's right shoulder. The engine was forced into the car and pinned his left leg and hit his stomach. The Hogans were trapped in the car for an hour. When doctors finally examined him, he had a broken collarbone, pelvis, ankle, and rib. He would live, but it was doubtful that he would play golf again.

Hogan made it his mission to return to golf. He started out slowly, chipping balls at Colonial Country Club in Fort Worth. By November, he was hitting full shots on the driving range. He played his first complete round of golf on December 10. When his entry into the 1950 Los Angeles Open was submitted, golf fans feared that Hogan was just chasing a dream and wouldn't even finish one round. The concern was valid, because Hogan's legs were still in bad shape. He couldn't play golf without wearing thick bandages from his ankles to his thighs. But Hogan was a survivor, and his courage overcame the agony of his battered legs.

Needless to say, the gallery was shocked when Hogan shot three consecutive 69s to post a 280. Sam Snead birdied the final two holes to tie Hogan. The 18-hole playoff was scheduled for a week later, after the Bing Crosby. Snead defeated Hogan, but his comeback is remembered as one of the greatest examples of athletic fortitude. Ironically, a few weeks later Hogan won the Sam Snead Festival at The Greenbrier with a record-tying 259. Hogan was back and Sam Snead couldn't do anything about it—even in the 1950 U.S. Open at Merion, which Hogan won. Hogan never won another tournament at Riviera, but the course will always be Hogan's Alley.

The expansive Riviera clubhouse, poised to overlook the course, was constructed in 1927.

THE COURSE

Riviera Country Club was moderately redesigned in 1993 by Ben Crenshaw. He concentrated on the greens to ensure that Tour players would have to putt well to win the L.A. Open. The course itself doesn't differ much from the 1927 Thomas–Bell design. Thomas was a wealthy Pennsylvania native who moved to California in 1919. He began designing golf courses as a hobby, but by the time the Los Angeles Athletic Club selected him to design their golf course in 1925 he had alrady designed two dozen others in California. Riviera was the last golf course he designed.

Thomas laid out the course in a small canyon dotted with trees. As the 20th century progressed, neighborhoods were developed to

Although the original forest has been replaced by real estate developments, Riviera's fairways are still lined with trees.

overlook the course. Although there are many holes at Riviera set away from the houses, they surround the entire club so that the nine holes comprising the outer circle of the layout have houses to the left and right and out of bounds. The trees play an important role, protecting fairways and greens and demanding accurate golf shots. Bunkers are another obstacle—there is no water on Riviera. Every hole has deep bunkers that snare slightly off-line shots and cause bogeys.

Although there are some hills on the Riviera course, they come into play on only a couple of holes. The 1st tee sits on top of a hill, making the par 5 play shorter than its 501 yards. This makes it a birdie hole, which is vital because the next three holes are par 4s over 400 yards, followed by a 238-yard par 3. The 447-yard, par-4 18th is one of the most famous holes

in golf. It is a sharp dogleg right with a blind tee shot up a hill. The slope of the fairway can cause a tee shot to dribble into the trees on the right, even a perfect tee shot doesn't promise safety. The green is surrounded by a huge bank filled with Kikuyu grass; any shot that misses the green sinks into the thick grass. Kikuyu grass, which plagues the entire course, has a thick surface that absorbs golf balls. Kikuyu is great fairway grass because the ball sits up nicely, but you don't want to encounter it in the rough.

It takes a great golfer like Ben Hogan to really succeed at Riviera. The Thomas–Bell design combined with Crenshaw's modified bunkers create a golf course where a pro golfer can experience one of the greatest moments of his career and an average golfer can taste the heritage of one of golf's most historic courses.

Galleries surround greens during the Los Angeles Open.

THE HISTORY

Scioto Country Club is a Donald Ross course that demands long tee shots. Jack Nicklaus was fortunate to learn to play golf on this course because it taught him to be a big hitter. Playing Scioto also familiarized Nicklaus with championship-caliber golf; the U.S. Open, Ryder Cup Match, and PGA Championship have all been held at Scioto. The 1926 Open, won by Bobby Jones, and the 1931 Ryder, won by the U.S., occurred before Nicklaus was born, but he was able to attend the 1950 PGA when he was ten years old.

Nicklaus must have learned a lot about tournament golf from that PGA. Among a field of such greats as Sam Snead, Gene Sarazen, Jimmy Demaret, Lloyd Mangrum, Henry Picard, and Bob Tomoski, the surprise victor was a little-known touring pro from Virginia named Chandler Harper. Harper defeated Henry Williams Jr. 4 and 3 in the finals to win his only career major. Witnessing underdog victories like this must have later given Nicklaus the inspiration to capture his first major win by defeating the favored Arnold Palmer in the 1962 U.S. Open.

Nicklaus's father, a Scioto member, introduced him to golf. Charles Nicklaus owned several pharmacies in Columbus. When Scioto's new pro, Jack Grout, came into Nicklaus Drug Store for some medication, Charles asked him about his junior golf program. Young Jack was so enthusiastic about taking up a new game—he was very athletic and later went on to play high school basketball—that he was the first to arrive at the pro shop for junior golf school and first on the tee box. He shot a 51 for nine holes and 91 overall, an impressive score for a ten-year-old who had never played before.

SCIOTO COUNTRY CLUB

•

Columbus, Ohio

•

6,901 yards, par 71

•

Designed by Donald Ross

•

Redesigned by Dick Wilson

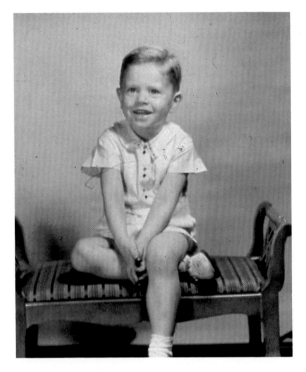

Jack Nicklaus got his start in golf as a young boy at Scioto.

Nicklaus was by far the most talented player in the junior golf school, and in less than a year under Grout's direction he shot an 81. Grout taught the young player many fundamentals of golf that helped form his great game. The first thing Grout stressed was keeping the head still through the entire swing to keep the balance on line after lifting the left foot onto the toe as the weight shifted onto the right foot. The next fundamental he stressed was a solid, full shoulder turn on the backswing. Both of these elements are now automatic to Nicklaus and an essential part of his successful swing.

When Nicklaus was 12, he broke 80 by shooting a 74, a great score for any golfer at Scioto. The next year, on a late summer afternoon, Nicklaus was playing a round with his father when he shot a 34 on the front nine. Because of the late hour, the pair was only planning to play nine but that would end Nick-

laus's chances of breaking 70 for the first time. So they went home for a quick meal and returned to play the back nine. Back then the 18th hole was a par 5, and Nicklaus needed an eagle to shoot a 69. After his drive, he hit a long iron onto the green 35 feet from the pin. Because it was almost completely dark, Nicklaus had difficulty reading the putt. Somehow, whether by talent or luck, he sunk the putt and broke 70 for the first time.

Between Grout and the Scioto course, Nicklaus became proficient at hitting a variety of shots. This advantage helped him win the Ohio State Open, won by other golf greats such as Byron Nelson and Tom Weiskopf, at age 16. When Nicklaus went to college at Ohio State University, he gave up basketball and devoted himself to golf. His game steadily improved at the collegiate level. He won his first out-of-state victory in the 1958 Trans-Miss Amateur and successfully defended his U.S. Amateur title in 1959 at Broadmoor East Course in Colorado. He also won the 1959 North and South Amateur at Pinehurst, a tournament his son would win in 1985. The following year he finished second in the U.S. Open at Cherry Hills.

Despite all of these victories, Nicklaus's best amateur year came in 1961. That year he won the U.S. Amateur at Pebble Beach, where he would later win one of his four U.S. Open titles, and his only NCAA individual title at Purdue Golf Course—Purdue won the team title. He also won the Western Amateur, which is a combination stroke- and match-play tournament, in 1961. As a result of these great amateur victories, Nicklaus turned pro in 1962 and launched an amazing professional career.

THE COURSE

A golfer has to play like Jack Nicklaus to post a good score at Scioto. Like any typical Donald Ross course, it has several small greens protected by bunkers and steep slopes. Only a perfect approach shot will stay on the green; most kick off into the sand or tall grass. The course Nicklaus learned to play on was altered dramatically in 1962, the year he turned pro. The par-5 18th he eagled to break 70 for the first time is now a 455-yard par 4. The par-5 tee was moved up and to the right, making it a straight hole toward a large green.

Some of the greatest changes were to the 505-yard, par-5 8th hole and the 209-yard, par-3 17th. In the original design a creek ran through Scioto, but it was converted to ponds on 8 and 17 in the redesign. The large pond on the 8th hole sits on the left side of the fairway 175 yards out and spreads up toward the green. There is a target area to the right of the pond but the creek traverses it just in front of the green. Pars and birdies require shots to

Only a long hitter can break 70 at Scioto.

COURSE RATING	Blue 73.8		White 71.5		Gold 69.3																			
SLOPE	140		134		131																			
HOLE	1	2	3	4	5	6	7	8	9	OUT	10	11	12	13	14	15	16	17	18	IN	OUT	Total	Hdcp	Net
BLUE COURSE	410	438	377	188	438	527	380	505	162	3425	424	365	545	435	238	408	425	191	445	3476	3425	6901		
WHITE COURSE	390	416	352	178	430	477	352	453	140	3188	405	348	505	412	195	362	400	163	420	3210	3188	6398		
GOLD COURSE	356	391	317	160	378	446	330	447	131	2956	384	330	488	379	178	340	378	147	400	3024	2956	5980		
STROKES	9	5	11	15	7	3	13	1	17		4	6	8	14	18	10	2	16	12					
PAR	4	4	4	3	4	5	4	5	3	36	4	4	5	4	3	4	4	3	4	35	36	71		
+ − 0																								

The water hazard makes the par-5 17th Scioto's signature hole.

stay on target, because hitting the water is common on 8. A similar pond was constructed on the site of the original 17th green. The new green is farther back and demands a 170-yard carry to stay dry.

Much of Ross's original design, such as his small greens, remains. His design combined with the length and ponds added makes Scioto a challenging course—even for the pros. It wouldn't hurt modern golfers to keep Grout's techniques in mind if they want to post a good score at Scioto.

Despite the fact that Sam Snead never won a U.S. Open, he is still considered the best golfer in history. This is mainly because he has set three PGA Tour records, all at Sedgefield Country Club. One of these records was set when he claimed his 81st Tour victory at Sedgefield. Jack Nicklaus has come closer than any other golfer to matching this record with 70 wins to his credit, but it is doubtful anyone else will come as close. Snead set another record by becoming the oldest player to win a PGA Tour event when he won the 1965 Greater Greensboro Open at age 52. Because of the success and the large purses in the Senior PGA Tour today, a golfer older than 52 will probably never play in a regular PGA Tour event again.

The Senior PGA Tour didn't exist in 1965. There was only one senior event in those days, the PGA Senior Championship, and Snead won it in 1964 and 1965. Since there was no other place for him to put his ageless golf swing to use, he had no other choice but to take on youngsters like Billy Casper, Tommy Aaron, Tony Lema, and Phil Rodgers. Anyone who watched Snead play in 1965 will remember that the 52-year-old's golf swing was just as limber as players twenty-five years his junior.

Snead recalls that week in April 1965 fondly because, in addition to his win, the tournament was dedicated to him. The week had been designated "Sam Snead Week" in honor of his previous seven wins at the Greater Greensboro Open, including a win at the first Open in 1938. When he sealed his eighth victory in 1965, he set another PGA record by becoming the only player to win a single Tour event eight times. The second-place record is

SEDGEFIELD COUNTRY CLUB

•

Greensboro, North Carolina

•

7,034 yards, par 71

•

Designed by Donald Ross

six wins set by Jack Nicklaus at the Masters, tied by Snead with six at the Miami Open. No current player is even within five wins of reaching Snead's record.

The dedication inspired Snead. "Oh, they had a big dinner for me and had Ed Sullivan emcee. He got up there and said, 'Wouldn't it be nice if Sam won?' That really inspired me to go out there and win," remembers Snead. He carded a 68 in the opening round, but it wasn't enough to take the lead. He followed with a 69 in the second round, which was enough to tie Casper at 137. A 68 on Saturday gave him a two-shot lead over rookie Labron Harris Jr., the 1962 U.S. Amateur champion. When the final round started, the younger players were determined to fight to the end. Phil Rodgers shot a 31 on the front nine to pull even with Snead at the turn. Tony Lema, playing ahead, had pulled within four but dropped a ball in the creek on 16. With Rodgers still in contention, Snead sunk a 60-foot birdie putt on the par-4 13th to gain a comfortable four-shot lead. "That putt was from China to Japan, but it won the tournament," said Snead.

He coasted in from the final round with a 68 to finish with a 273 and a five-shot win. Snead said of the $11,000 first-place check, "Heck, that was more than I made at Greensboro in my life, and it was one of the biggest checks I had ever won." In fact, it was almost more than what he had won for his seven previous wins combined, which totalled only $13,900. The 1965 Greater Greensboro Open was his last PGA Tour win. It was appropriate that it came on a course he dominated for so many years.

Sam Snead won the Greater Greensboro Open in 1965 before the Senior PGA Tour was formed.

THE COURSE

Snead's success in the Greater Greensboro Open is due in part to the fact that his game is well suited to the Sedgefield course. His ability to hit long tee shots, for example, helped on the 7,034-yard long course. It's also hilly, resembling the Cascades course in Hot Springs, Virginia, where Snead turned pro. It has many up-and-down holes as well as natural mounds off the sides of greens.

The North Carolina setting also provides a lot of trees and water. Snead was able to maneuver past these obstacles because he is a long, accurate hitter. Length, however, isn't always the problem. The most troublesome hole at

Sedgefield is the par-3 16th, which is only 159 yards long. It is a classic par 3 with a creek running in front of the tiny green. Golfers going for the pin often fall short and splash down into the creek.

Par is another factor that increases Sedgefield's difficulty. Because it is only 71, there are 11 long par 4s, all over 400 yards long. This is another reason Snead played the course so well. It's an all-around tough course, but a long hitter certainly has the advantage.

◀ All of the par 4s on this 7,034-yard course are over 400 yards long.

▼ The clubhouse was built in 1926, just one year after the club was chartered.

◀ Sedgefield's rolling landscape provides a variety of uphill and downhill holes.

SHINNECOCK HILLS GOLF CLUB

•

Southampton, New York

•

6,697 yards, par 70

•

Designed by Willie Dunn

•

Redesigned by Dick Wilson

After the Apple Tree Gang at St. Andrews established golf in the United States, interest in the game increased among affluent New York residents. Several wealthy New Yorkers were visiting Biarritz, a famous French spa, in 1889 when they met Willie Dunn, a Scottish golf professional who was designing the spa's golf course. They asked Dunn to teach them the game of golf. He gave them a lesson, and they enjoyed the game so much that they asked Dunn to lay out a golf course on some land on Long Island.

William Vanderbilt, one of those three Americans, was convinced that golf would catch on quickly in the U.S. Together with Edward Mead, Thomas Barber, George Schieffelin, and Duncan Cryder, Vanderbilt decided to form a golf club near the Hamptons. Dunn arrived in New York in March 1891 and immediately set about searching for links land on which he could construct a course. He and Samuel Parrish, one of the club's founders, discovered an area called Shinnecock Hills overlooking the Peconic Bay near Southampton. Dunn was excited to see the rolling, bushy, Scottish-links-type land on Long Island. Dunn hired 150 Native Americans from the Shinnecock reservation to do the construction. By fall the 12-hole course was open, and the members asked Dunn to construct a 9-hole ladies course. Although the ladies course never came to be, Dunn expanded the original course to 18 holes the next year. Noted architect William Flynn was hired to redesign the course in 1931, but one of his employees, Dick Wilson, actually did the work.

Because the membership would consist of wealthy people, the golf course had to be top-notch; equally important was the quality of the clubhouse. The Shinnecock Hills club-house was designed by the famous architect Standford White. He designed a luxurious structure that attracted many of the club's original members. Interest in the club was strong, and a waiting list for those who wished to join Shinnecock Hills had to be created. The standards established by the club's board of directors were so good that other golf clubs forming at the time used them to set up their new clubs.

When the need was recognized for an organized golf association, Shinnecock's key members were invited to meet with members of St. Andrews, The Country Club at Brookline, Newport Country Club, and Chicago Golf Club to form the USGA. Because Shinnecock

Hills was so much like a Scottish links course and a cofounder of the USGA, the club was chosen to host the second USGA national championship in 1896. The U.S. Amateur was more prestigious than the U.S. Open because pros were considered blue-collar workers. Defending Amateur champion Charles Blair MacDonald, from Chicago, was defeated in match play. The winner was another Chicagoan, H.J. Whigham, who emigrated from England. After defeating J.G. Thorp 8 and 7, he moved back to Chicago and married MacDonald's daughter.

▸ *Although women golfers were rare around 1900, they were welcome at Shinnecock Hills.*

▾ *A circle drive was all the parking lot needed for the horse-drawn carriages of the early 1900s.*

The Open, 36 holes with only 35 players, was won by another Chicago native, Jim Foulis. Foulis was a Scottish immigrant hired by Mac-Donald as a pro at Chicago Golf Club. He shot 78-74—152 to win by three shots over defending champion Horace Rawlins. The final-round 74 set a tournament record that stood until Willie Anderson shot a 72 in the 1904 Open at Glen View Club in Illinois.

The U.S. Open didn't return to Shinnecock Hills until 1986, mainly because golf was growing so quickly in the United States that there were more and more quality golf courses to choose from. When the 1977 Walker Cup match was staged at Shinnecock Hills, USGA Executive Director Frank Hannigan decided to bring the Open back.

Raymond Floyd won his only career Open in 1986 at Shinnecock Hills. He closed in with a final-round 66 to win by two strokes over Lanny Wadkins and Chip Beck, both of whom finished with final-round 65s. Greg Norman started the "Third Round Grand Slam" at the Masters that year, where he was the leader but didn't win. He also led the third rounds of the Open at Shinnecock Hills, the British Open at Turnberry, and the PGA at Inverness. He won only the British Open but became the only golfer ever to lead the third rounds of all four majors in the same year. The USGA will return to Shinnecock Hills for the centennial year of the U.S. Open in 1995.

THE COURSE

Like links courses in Scotland, the wind is a major factor at Shinnecock Hills. It makes the 6,697-yard course play like 7,000 yards. Every short par 4 is laid out to play into the wind; the long ones play downwind. This is not so bad when the wind is blowing from the southwest as it normally does. However, when the wind comes in from the northeast, the long par 4s are virtually unreachable in regulation. For example, the 470-yard, par-4 12th hole is playable downwind but

	Westward Ho	Plateau	Peconic	Pump House	Montauk	The Pond	Redan	Lowlands	Ben Nevis	Out		Eastward Ho	Hill Head	Tuckahoe	Road Side	Thom's Elbow	Sebonac	Shinnecock	Eden	Home	In	Total
Hole	1	2	3	4	5	6	7	8	9			10	11	12	13	14	15	16	17	18		
Red	391	221	456	409	529	456	184	361	411	3418		412	158	469	372	447	400	542	169	426	3395	6813
Green	380	193	422	373	487	415	173	319	373	3135		402	150	427	354	436	357	464	149	374	3113	6248
White	366	146	395	303	413	368	133	281	307	2712		337	121	396	325	361	288	406	140	289	2663	5375
Par	4	3	4	4	5	4	3	4	4	35		4	3	4	4	4	4	5	3	4	35	70
Strokes	11	17	3	7	9	1	15	13	5			4	16	2	12	6	14	8	18	10		

SHINNECOCK HILLS GOLF CLUB

▲ *Shinnecock Hills boasts the oldest clubhouse in America.*
▶ *The Long Island location of Shinnecock Hills was chosen because of its hilly landscape and view of Peconic Bay.*

should almost be converted to a par 5 into the wind. With seven bunkers in front of the green, a second shot that can't reach the green lands in the beach.

There are no water hazards at Shinnecock Hills, making it even more like a standard Scottish links course. Every hole is packed with bunkers that require a solid approach shot to hit the green. The 159-yard, par-3 11th hole is a typical bunker-dominated hole. It plays downwind, but the tee shot has to be dead solid perfect to carry all four bunkers in front of the green. Good tee shots are essential to a successful round at Shinnecock Hills. Like all true links land, there are mounds on the fairways that were created by winds blowing off the ocean for centuries. Shinnecock Hills provides an authentic links experience to the American golfer.

SIWANOY COUNTRY CLUB

•

Bronxville, New York

•

6,359 yards, par 71

•

Designed by Donald Ross

THE HISTORY

Golf courses were popping up all over the United States in the first two decades of the 20th century. Most were private clubs, and many of them hired golf professionals from Scotland who immigrated to the U.S. in hopes of making money. These immigrants were considered nothing more than blue-collar workers. A golf pro's duties consisted of taking care of the golf course, repairing and making golf clubs, handling tournaments, overseeing the other golf employees, and serving members. The best pros made only $50 a week. The affluent club members viewed the pros as employees, not fellow golfers. The pro wasn't even allowed in the clubhouse—that's why pro shops were constructed as separate buildings away from the clubhouse.

In the Gay Nineties, a Professional Golfers Association was formed in England to ensure that British and Scottish golf pros were treated well by the clubs. When Scottish pros informed the American pros of this association, they decided to form their own PGA in America. The PGA of America gave the pros a tournament to play in—the majority of the tournaments back then were held for amateurs. Even the USGA was reluctant to include pros in tournaments. However, they added the U.S. Open to give pros a tournament, even though the amateurs were considered the better players.

The formation of the PGA of America came about at the suggestion of Tom McNamara, a former caddie and a salesman for Rodman Wanamaker's pro golf department in Philadelphia. An organizing committee met on January 24, 1916, at Taplow Club in New York to outline a PGA constitution using the British PGA constitution as their model. On February

24, the constitution and bylaws were approved. On that day, 35 golf pros became charter members of the PGA of America. In April, 92 applicants from around the country applied for membership. Seventy-eight were accepted, and groups were eventually formed in all states. Robert White, head pro at Wykagyl Country Club in New York, was named PGA president. By June, 139 more members were added. A tournament committee was formed to plan a national PGA Championship where pros could compete against each other rather than amateurs. This was important considering three of the previous four U.S. Open champions had been amateurs.

The first PGA National Championship was scheduled for October 9, 1916, at Siwanoy Country Club, a course north of Manhattan Island that was converted from a 9-hole course in Mount Vernon to a Donald Ross-designed 18-hole course in Bronxville. The PGA chose Siwanoy because it was difficult enough to challenge the pros. The tournament was planned as a 36-hole match play, because that was the traditional style of national tournaments in Europe. Wanamaker supported golf professionals, who were the main customers of his golf department. He donated a trophy, a diamond medal for the winner, a gold medal for the runner-up, and silver medals for the qualifying round winners. He also provided the $2,500 purse.

Thirty-one pros qualified for the first PGA. The favorite was Walter Hagen, winner of the 1914 U.S. Open. Long Jim Barnes, a 6-foot-4 Scottish immigrant working in San Francisco, and Jock Hutchison, a St. Andrews native, were two others to watch. Thomas Kerrigan, the head pro at Siwanoy, hit the first shot in the PGA Championship. He teed off in a match with Charles Adams, which he won 6

and 4. Hagen won his first match 7 and 6 over J.R. Thomson; Barnes won 8 and 7 over George Fortheringham; and Hutchison won 11 and 9 over Joe Mitchell. All four won their second rounds—another 11 and 9 win for Hutchison. Hutchison looked like the best player in the tournament, but anything can happen in match play. Barnes shot the lowest score in the championship when he posted a first-round 71 to set up his 3 and 1 victory over Kerrigan; he beat Willie MacFarlane 6 and 5 to make the final-round match. Hutchison defeated Hagen 2-up to face Barnes in the finals. It looked like Hutchison was going to win. He was 3-up after the first nine holes, shooting a 37 to Barnes's 39. Barnes narrowed the lead to 1-up after the first 18 holes—both players shot 77.

After a lunch break, Barnes told the gallery, "I always do better after lunch." And he did. The match was squared on the 3rd hole, a 206-yard par 3. Barnes sank an 18-foot birdie putt on the 371-yard, par-4 7th to take a 1-up lead. Both players sunk 35-foot birdie putts on the

A sign on the 18th fairway honors Siwanoy as the site of the first PGA.

293-yard, par-4 9th to tie the hole. Barnes continued his streak by holing a 25-foot birdie on the 362-yard, par-4 10th to go 2-up. Hutchison kept on grinding. On the 197-yard, par-3 11th, he made a 15-foot birdie putt to go only 1-down. When he parred the 188-yard, par-3 13th, he was even with Barnes. The 531-yard, par-5 18th hole would determine the winner. They both played the hole well, lofting their approach shots five feet from the pin. The putts had to be measured to see who was away. Hutchison was one inch farther out and lipped out the putt. The pressure to win the first PGA was high as Barnes rolled in his putt to win 1-up.

The exposure of the PGA helped both Barnes and Hutchison. Barnes won $500, and Hutchison won $250. The money was nice, but what was more important was that the major championship influenced the future for the Scottish players. The PGA Championship and all other tournaments were cancelled the next

two years because of World War I. Barnes successfully defended his title in 1919 at Engineers Country Club on Long Island. He went on to win the 1921 U.S. Open at Columbia Country Club in Chevy Chase, Maryland. Hutchison finally won the PGA in 1920 at Flossmoor Country Club in Chicago, and, in 1921, he won the British Open in his hometown of St. Andrews. The first PGA at Siwanoy Country Club paved the way for future pros to play in tournaments and earn the respect they deserve.

THE COURSE

Golfers playing Siwanoy Country Club today play virtually the same course that launched the PGA Championship. The 6,359-yard course was a formidable challenge because shots hit with hickory-shaft clubs traveled about 20 percent shorter than they do with modern steel and graphite shafts.

The clubhouse that members enjoy today was rebuilt in the spring of 1929.

Siwanoy is not as monstrous now as it was back then, but it's still not easy. The clubhouse sits on top of a Bronxville hill, and the course rolls up and down around it. This makes it play much longer than the yardage listing. Another element that raises scores at Siwanoy is the firm, undulating greens. Shots often bounce off the Donald Ross greens into bunkers. Ross required approach shots to be right on line to stay on the green, a prerequisite for birdies and pars.

In addition to the greens, the hilly landscape tests golfers' patience. The 511-yard, par-5 5th hole, for example, can only be birdied by top-rate golfers—average golfers get into trouble quickly. The downhill tee shot leads to a second shot over a creek that cuts across the fairway 100 yards in front of the green. Not only must the shot carry the creek but it must also bounce up a hill between sand traps to reach the green.

Sand traps are the standard hazards of the early 20th century. The 293-yard 9th hole, Siwanoy's shortest par 4, is a classic early-century hole. All levels of golfers can reach the green in regulation, but the approach shot has to be perfect to avoid a bogey or double bogey. The small green rests on a hill surrounded by five sand traps. The semiblind approach shot prevents golfers from seeing the pin location. The tiny, bunkered green is a typical Ross design.

Golfers playing the par-5 18th hole have to go for broke to clear the creek.

Trees protect the 362-yard, par-4 10th hole and kill slices. A creek swallows tee shots on the 358-yard, par-4 12th hole and comes back into play on the 531-yard, par-5 18th. Eighteen is a lot like 5, where golfers have to either boom it over the creek or layup. In both cases, the creek comes into play.

With so many natural hazards and an extraordinary Donald Ross design, it is only fitting that the first PGA championship was staged at Siwanoy Country Club. Golf is not the same game it was in 1916, but those natural hazards make the course one of the most arduous short courses in America.

SOUTHERN HILLS COUNTRY CLUB

•

Tulsa, Oklahoma

•

6,931 yards, par 71

•

Designed by Perry Maxwell

There have been numerous major championships played south of the Mason-Dixon Line, but most majors are held only once or twice on Southern golf courses. However, with seven USGA majors and three PGA Championships, including the 1994 PGA, Southern Hills Country Club in Tulsa, Oklahoma, is the premier major championship golf course in the South.

One of the reasons Southern Hills is considered one of the best golf courses in the South is its resemblance to the great golf courses of the Northeast and Upper Midwest. Its success is due in part to its foundation of oil wealth. Southern Hills was formed in 1935, during the Great Depression, when oil millionaire Waite Phillips and his fellow oil millionaires decided to develop a country club. Obviously, they were weathering the Depression well. Along with Augusta National, Southern Hills was the greatest golf course developed during the Great Depression. Equally impressive as its excellence is the fact that Southern Hills even survived the era that witnessed the collapse of country clubs across the U.S.

Southern Hills's first major was the 1946 USGA Women's Amateur, where Babe Didrickson Zaharias won her first national title. She turned pro when the Women's Professional Golf Association, which later evolved into the LPGA, was formed. In 1953, the USGA staged the Boys' Junior Championship, won by Rex Baxter Jr., at Southern Hills. The success of those two national championships convinced the USGA to schedule the 1958 U.S. Open at Southern Hills.

Many of the Open players were surprised at how difficult the course was. After Gene Sara-

▲ *Southern Hills has hosted more majors than any other golf club in the South.*
▶ *The par-4 12th green is the most difficult to hit in regulation.*

zen shot an 84 in the first round, he called the course "ridiculous." But he wasn't the only one to play over par. Ben Hogan shot a 75, as did Sam Snead. Snead shot a second-round 80 and missed the U.S. Open cut for the first time in his career. Not a single golfer broke par in the first round. The player leading the pack was native Oklahoman Tommy Bolt. He shot a one-over par 71 in the first round to tie Julius Boros and Dick Metz. Bolt, who was used to playing in the 90-degree heat and on bermuda grass, shot another 71 to take a one-stroke lead over a 22-year-old South African named Gary Player. Bolt remained consistent, shooting 69-72 on the 36-hole final day. Even though he was three over par in the tournament, he succeeded in winning the U.S. Open by four shots over Player.

The USGA decided that the source of such a high winning score must be a true championship course. It returned in 1961 with the Senior

Amateur, which was won by Dexter Daniels. Four years later the USGA staged the first stroke play U.S. Amateur at Southern Hills. Stroke play, as opposed to match play, became the standard in golf because so many amateurs were turning to the PGA Tour after winning the U.S. Amateur. By this time, the PGA Championship had gone to stroke play, and there wasn't a single match-play event left on the PGA Tour. College events were also turning to stroke play. The stroke-play U.S. Amateur lasted only eight years. When a native New York athlete named Bob Murphy injured his

shoulder playing baseball for the University of Florida, he went back to his first love, golf. He traveled to the U.S. Amateur at Southern Hills and won by shooting a 72-hole score of 291, one stroke ahead of Bob Dickson. That was the only U.S. Amateur ever held at Southern Hills, but its stroke-play format fit well with the course layout.

In 1970, Southern Hills was chosen to host the PGA Championship. Bob Murphy, who had turned pro by then, was in the field along with Arnold Palmer, Jack Nicklaus, Gary Player, Lee Trevino, Hale Irwin, Doug Sanders, Deane Beman and many other golf greats. Murphy may not have been famous, but he had talent. The player to watch out for was Dave Stockton, a 28-year-old California native. Stockton came out of the pack with a third-round 66 and a three-stroke lead. In the final round, he held off a classic Arnold Palmer charge. Another player who came charging up was Murphy, who also shot a 66. But that wasn't good enough to win. Stockton closed with a 279, the lowest Southern Hills winning score. Palmer and Murphy finished two shots back.

The 1977 Open at Southern Hills was by far their most unusual major. Hubert Green, the 1971 PGA Tour Rookie of the Year, was an Alabama native who knew how to play golf in hot weather. He played well and was the third-round leader with a 208. There was no longer a 36-hole final day by then, so the final round was on Sunday. Green was paired with another Southern golfer, Andy Bean, who was one stroke behind Green. Green moved well ahead of Bean on the front nine. By the time

The high temperatures and thick bermuda grass give native Southerners an advantage in major championships.

SOUTHERN HILLS COUNTRY CLUB

The par-4 2nd hole is an excellent example of Southern Hills's tree-lined fairways that demand straight shots.

Green and Bean stepped onto the 10th tee, a Tulsa police lieutenant informed the USGA that a clerk in the FBI Oklahoma City office had received a call from a woman claiming three men were on their way to Southern Hills to kill Green. At first, the police didn't tell Green he was under a death threat, but they did send extra officers to the course. That made Green nervous and could have cost him the Open, especially since Lou Graham was playing well on the back nine. Graham, the 1975 Open champion, birdied four out of five holes to pull within one stroke of Green. On the 17th, Graham hooked his tee shot into the trees and made a dramatic recovery shot with a 3-iron that skipped onto the green only eight feet from the cup. Luckily for Green, he missed the putt.

At the time Graham was putting on 17, a police lieutenant called Green aside as he walked off the 14th green and told him about the death threat. Green could either withdraw from the Open, ask for play to be suspended, or keep on playing. Green opted to keep on playing because he thought the death threat was a sick joke from an ex-girlfriend. He continued to play well, making a birdie on 16 and sinking a 50-foot putt for par on 17. He hit his second shot on 18 into the bunker, chopped the ball out 20-feet short, and hit his putt three-and-a-half feet short of the cup. Fortunately, he made it to win by one stroke over Graham with a 278, the lowest winning score to be posted at Southern Hills. Apparently, the death threat was a joke. Although he hasn't won a tournament since the 1985 PGA Cham-

pionship, he still plays on the PGA Tour at age 47.

The last time a PGA was staged at Southern Hills was 1982. Raymond Floyd was having a winning season when he arrived at the PGA Championship. He had already won two tournaments and was second on the money list. He shot a first-round 63 to tie the PGA Championship low 18-hole score set by Bruce Crampton in 1975 at Firestone; it was also the lowest first-round score ever recorded by a PGA winner. Floyd cruised through Southern Hills. He

176

HISTORIC GOLF COURSES OF AMERICA

led all four rounds, defeating Lanny Wadkins by three strokes after shooting a final-round 72, his first round at Southern Hills over 70. He certainly made the course look easier than Gene Sarazen and his contemporaries.

THE COURSE

The way Floyd, Green, Bolt, Murphy, and Stockton managed to win at Southern Hills was by hitting the ball dead solid perfect—particularly off the tee. Tee shots are the foundation of a good round at Southern Hills because every hole has a narrow fairway lined with trees. The infamous bermuda grass is another burden that irritates non-Southern players. It produces extremely thick rough, which becomes the USGA half-stroke penalty because it is often impossible to hit the second shot onto the green due to a deep lie. In fact, the rough is so thick that Ben Hogan injured his wrists playing in the 1958 Open and was forced to withdraw. He had gotten to play the entire course earlier and considers the 445-yard, par-4 12th hole one of the toughest par

4s he has ever played. It is a long dogleg left with a narrow downhill fairway that ends at a green encompassed by trees, bunkers, and a creek. Most golfers choose to layup with their second shot—if the tee shot falls into the sand trap at the left corner of the dogleg or in the rough, it's no longer a choice.

Although the 12th is easy to double bogey, the most difficult hole is the 430-yard, par-4 18th. The creek on the 12th hole veers slightly onto the left side of the 18th fairway. The second shot has to climb a hill to reach the green. There are two bunkers in the fairway about 160 yards short of the green and two more immediately in front of the green on the side of the hill. The green is practically impossible to reach in regulation, even if the tee shot is dead solid perfect. The other 16 holes at Southern Hills are equally challenging. Ben Crenshaw recently designed nine new holes away from the tournament 18 to provide a more relaxing round of golf for the members. As the most frequent Southern host of major championships, a round of golf at Southern Hills provides golfers with the experience of quality golf.

THE HISTORY

S t. Andrews Golf Club is the oldest existing golf club in the United States. When John Reid, the "father of American golf," founded the golf club in New York, he laid the foundation for golf in the United States. Although the extinct Oakhurst Links was officially the first golf club, it did not increase the game's popularity as St. Andrews did.

Reid learned to play golf while growing up in Scotland. When he was old enough to seek his fortune, he immigrated to the U.S. He got a job with J.L. Mott Iron Works, where he soon became an executive, and by 1880 he was financially strong. In 1887 Reid commissioned Robert Lockhart, a man from his hometown of Dumferlime, to acquire a set of six golf clubs and two dozen gutta percha balls. Lockhart purchased the equipment from Tom Morris's golf shop in St. Andrews. Because there was nowhere for him to play, Reid set up a 3-hole course on a cow pasture he owned in Westchester County. Reid hadn't planned on playing until the spring, but on February 22, 1888 the weather was sunny and clear, so he invited a few friends over to join him in his native game. The course wasn't elaborate, just a field with cups cut in the ground, but it was enough for his friends to become interested in the game.

A few weeks after the group played for the first time a blizzard hit New York, and it was several months before they could play again. By that time, they were eager to expand the course to six holes. The group located some land, owned by a butcher named John C. Shotts, on the southeast corner of North Broadway and Shonnard Place in Yonkers. Reid and his friends played throughout the summer and fall. On November 14, he invited his friends to his

ST. ANDREWS GOLF CLUB

•

Hastings-on-Hudson, New York

•

6,616 yards, par 71

•

Designed by William H. Tucker

•

Redesigned by James Baird and Jack Nicklaus

The Clubhouse of The Apple Tree Gang 1888

Under this tree, still alive and sturdy at 626 Palisade Avenue, Yonkers, the founders of St. Andrew's planned the golf conquest of America.

▼ *The clubhouse of the modern St. Andrews was built in the 1930s.*

home for dinner, and there they decided to form a golf club to be named St. Andrews after the famous Scottish course.

At that time there was no clubhouse, just the field. By 1892 the membership had risen to thirteen. The members were playing so frequently that they were outgrowing their 6-hole course. There was a proposal to expand the course to nine holes, but Reid was not interested. Ironically, by that time it was no longer "his club," so he had to go along with it. The course couldn't be expanded where it was because the city of Yonkers was extending Palisades Avenue north. It was to cut through the golf course, which the city had no use for, so the club was forced to relocate once again.

St. Andrews's new site was four blocks north in an apple orchard. Residents near the new course labeled the golfers the "Apple Tree Gang," because they looked ridiculously out of

place hitting golf balls around apple trees. They still didn't have a clubhouse, but the members set a chair under an apple tree near the first tee. This area functioned as their clubhouse. They would lay their coats on the crouch of the tree and hang their lunch baskets on the limbs. After a round, the players would gather in the shade of the tree and sit down for a relaxing picnic.

By 1894, the popularity of golf had grown in the U.S., and St. Andrews's membership had reached 20. At the same time, Shinnecock Hills, a new 9-hole course on Long Island, replaced St. Andrews as the country's best golf course. It had a stately clubhouse and a links-style course designed by Willie Dunn. The Apple Tree Gang recognized that they were falling behind and wanted to raise their club to the new standards of golf. The first thing they did was hire a Scottish pro named Samuel Tucker; they also hired his brother, Willie, to lay out a 9-hole course. This time the club relocated to Grey Oaks, three miles north of the Apple Tree Course. The layout only took a few days, and the club reopened on May 11, 1894.

When Charles Blair MacDonald caused the stir in 1894 that formed the USGA, he was playing tournaments at Newport Golf Club and St. Andrews. After taking a first-round lead in the national championship at Newport with an 89, he skied to 100 in the second round. His ball lodged against a stone wall, which was a popular hazard in those days. The wall caused him to lose the tournament to W.G. Lawrence, a Newport member. MacDonald erupted and loudly refused to recognize Lawrence as the winner. He made it clear to everyone within earshot that stroke play was not the way to determine a national champion. The Scottish relied on match play, and MacDonald was convinced that was the only way to name a true champion.

Despite his outlandish behavior, enough people agreed with him to hold another tournament. The next month St. Andrews hosted a match-play championship. MacDonald held a strong lead after the first two rounds, but stayed out the second night until five in the morning guzzling champagne with Stanford White, the architect of Madison Square Garden. When he

realized he was due to tee off in two hours, he took a short nap, downed some pep pills, and took his revenge on Lawrence by defeating him 2 and 1.

Not surprisingly, MacDonald wasn't feeling well by lunchtime. White, who was in the gallery, suggested a rare steak and a bottle of champagne as a remedy. So, armed with one hour's sleep, a rare steak in his stomach, and more than enough champagne, MacDonald headed back to the tournament to face Laurence Stoddard. They were even after 18 holes. On the first playoff hole, a woozy MacDonald sliced his tee shot into an adjacent field. It took him three strokes to get back on the course, and, by then, Stoddard had secured the win.

Of course, MacDonald was furious about losing the national championship. This time he argued that the title was invalid because the tournament wasn't governed by a ruling body such as the Royal and Ancient Golf Club of St. Andrews. Once again, as boorishly as MacDonald was behaving, his fellow golfers agreed with the need for standardized rules of golf. John Reid and Henry O. Tallmadge, another

The first photo of a golf game played in the United States was taken in 1888 on St. Andrews's original course.

St. Andrews member, went to the Calmut Club in New York to meet with members from the Newport Golf Club, The Country Club in Brookline, Shinnecock Hills, and the Chicago Golf Club. Together these five clubs formed the Amateur Golf Association of the United States. Other clubs were also invited to join the association, which later changed its name to the United States Golf Association because of its dealings with golf professionals. Tallmadge was named secretary and spent much of his time organizing the USGA and setting up national tournaments.

Three years later, St. Andrews moved for the last time to its present location at Mt. Hope on the Hudson River. This location had enough land available for an 18-hole course and was accessible to members from Manhattan by train. If it hadn't been for Reid and the Apple Tree Gang founding St. Andrews Golf Club, golf may never have never gained widespread popularity in the United States.

THE COURSE

I f the Apple Tree Gang was alive today, they would have trouble recognizing the modern St. Andrews course. The course they played on wasn't much more than grass and a few trees. When Jack Nicklaus redesigned it, he modernized it by adding several water hazards, more trees, and plenty of bunkers. This challenging new version of the course includes many holes that embrace every penalty possibility in golf. Although Nicklaus's design is only 6,616 yards, he created some new holes that demand perfect shots to avoid disaster.

The ultimate Nicklaus hole at St. Andrews is the 520-yard, par-5 11th. Set away from the original course, the hole flies down hill to a narrow green that is surrounded by rocks and out of bounds. Even long hitters have difficulty reaching the green in two because it's so small. The 11th can kill a decent round.

Located below luxury condos, St. Andrews's 18th green is practically an automatic three-putt.

	HOLE	MEN BACK	MEN MIDDLE	MEN FORWARD	STROKES	SELF	P'TNER	OPP'T	OPP'T	PAR	WOMEN STROKES	WOMEN FORWARD				
REID'S GATE	1	341	306	256	11					4	11	228				
GILLIE'S FARM	2	340	326	320	15					4	13	302				
RED OAK	3	179	165	149	17					3	15	132				
VALLEY VIEW	4	414	399	392	3					4	5	327				
BURNSIDE	5	196	173	165	13					3	17	114				
THE LOCH	6	423	401	366	9					4	7	316				
LONGFELLOW	7	547	516	493	7					5	1	453				
ROAD HOLE	8	457	422	382	1					4	9	308				
HALFWAY	9	574	547	507	5					5	3	408				
	OUT	3471	3255	3030						36		2588				
PLAYER											INITIALS					
CARNEGIE HILL	10	315	286	275	10					4	12	260				
CEMETERY	11	531	491	481	2					5	2	437				
THE ROCKS	12	135	115	115	18					3	18	110				
FOX HILL	13	209	196	185	14					3	16	146				
TASSIE	14	414	394	350	12					4	6	344				
TWIN LAKES	15	397	384	374	6					4	8	334				
JACK'S GLEN	16	176	148	140	16					3	14	130				
LONE PINE	17	525	483	475	8					5	4	447				
HOME	18	443	381	364	4					4	10	338				
	IN	3145	2878	2759						35		2546				
	TOT	6616	6133	5789						71		5134				
HANDICAP												DATE				
NET SCORE																
SCORER							ATTESTED									

▲ *The par-3 16th is short but often bogeyed.*
▶ *A tee shot on the 4th flies downhill to a target fairway.*

Many of the St. Andrews members were displeased with the Nicklaus design and requested alterations. The 1st hole, a sharp dogleg left, was a major point of contention. Most members couldn't hit a playable tee shot because the dogleg was at such a severe angle that the ball landed in the trees almost every time. St. Andrews eventually reopened the original 1st hole and converted Nicklaus's to a driving range.

One great improvement Nicklaus made was on the 412-yard, par-4 4th hole. The original layout was only about 330 yards long and was a straight shot from the tee, which sat atop a 150-foot hill. Nicklaus kept the basic design of the tee and fairway but cut down some trees to the left and built a small, undulating green just past a new creek. The original hole was challenging for hickory shaft players, and Nicklaus's conversion made it equally difficult for steel and graphite shaft players.

The greens at St. Andrews test even the most accurate putters. Like the new 4th hole, undulations characterize most greens. These undulations are so severe that they might be more appropriately described as hills and val-leys. They make three-putts common for all levels of golfers.

Another hazard frequently encountered at St. Andrews is water. Nicklaus added ponds and creeks in his redesign for irrigation and to make the course more demanding. The 537-yard 7th hole, a par 5, already had one creek, Span Brook Creek, when Nicklaus added two more. The creek just in front of the tee doesn't cause many problems, but the other one is only fifty yards short of Span Brook. A golfer has to lay-up short of this creek because the second shot has to clear both. The area between the two creeks is deep rough, so the shot has to be long enough to carry the first creek, the rough, and then Span Brook.

Among the hundreds of willows scattered over St. Andrews are a few remaining apple trees. They stand as reminders of the men who popularized golf in America.

TPC SAWGRASS

•

Ponte Vedra, Florida

•

6,857 yards, par 72

•

Designed by Pete Dye

TPC Sawgrass, opened in 1980, is the youngest historic golf course in the U.S. What makes it historic is its status as the first Tournament Players club course opened by the PGA Tour. The PGA Tour formed TPC courses in response to the growing popularity of PGA Tour events. Nearly all PGA Tour events have title and corporate sponsors. These sponsors need a lot of space to entertain their clients. Before the TPC concept, most courses on the Tour were country clubs or public courses set up for golf only. This didn't leave enough land for sponsor cabins to be set up alongside the course, making it more difficult for the PGA to attract a wide variety of sponsors. TPC courses are designed with sponsor cabin communities in mind.

The lack of space was also a problem for the gallery. The golf boom of the late 1970s resulted in more people attending PGA Tour events. Golf is the only sport in the world that is easier to watch on television than in person. Only hard-core golfers are willing to hike five miles, dodge hundreds of spectators, and endure obstructed views to catch a glimpse of their favorite pros. The average golfer and the casual fan would just as soon stay home and watch the tournament on TV. TPCs are stadium-course designs with large mounds that allow for a greater number of spectators and provide a better view of greens, fairways, and tees. Some mounds even feature permanent seats, which makes watching a Tour event more like watching an NFL game from the 50-yard line. Because of the improved conditions, more spectators are buying tickets to PGA Tour events. For example, when the Shell Houston Open moved from The Woodlands's West

Course to the TPC at The Woodlands in 1985, the average number of spectators increased from 85,000 to 175,000.

TPC courses will be the foundation of the PGA Tour in the 21st century. One reason, in addition to the increased sponsor space and gallery accommodations, is the difficulty of TPC courses. PGA Tour players are the best golfers in the world, so it is only fitting that they play on courses that are even more challenging than standard club courses. TPC courses are designed to remain challenging to a 21st-century PGA player who is likely to hit a tee shot 325 yards, or 380 if he's a big hitter. It's possible that TPC courses will one day become the only golf courses on the PGA Tour.

TPC at Sawgrass opened under controversial conditions. Pete Dye, the course designer, is known for laying out the most difficult courses in the world. He is an advocate of target golf, which requires golfers to hit straight shots a precise distance to reach fairways and greens while avoiding nearby hazards. When the Tournament Players Championship (now called The Players Championship) moved to TPC Sawgrass in 1982, many of the Tour players were upset with the extreme difficulty of the course. A major point of contention was the severity of the undulating greens. Three-putting was almost too common, and players were frustrated with making bogeys after hitting great shots to reach the green.

In 1982, the first Tournament Players Championship at the TPC at Sawgrass was won by Jerry Pate, the 1976 U.S. Open champion. Although his score wasn't great, he was pleased with the TPC win, which turned out to be his last in a professional tournament. After signing his scorecard, Pate returned to the 18th green and tossed PGA Tour Commissioner Deane Be-

Hooking a second shot into the water on 18 can cost a golfer The Players Championship.

man and Pete Dye into the pond beside the green. Pate dove in after them and joined the underwater celebration. The success of the Tournament Players Championship at Sawgrass enabled the PGA to apply the TPC concept to other Tour events. The PGA Tour established PGA Tour Investments, Inc. to invest with real estate developers who were interested in constructing TPC courses. Because of the connection with the PGA Tour, TPC developers were able to use famous Tour players as design consultants. In some instances, golf clubs and resorts that wanted a TPC course but didn't want the PGA Tour to co-own the course were able to purchase a TPC license. Since the opening of TPC at Sawgrass there have been 20 more TPC courses designed or contracted to host PGA Tour and Senior PGA Tour events. As they continue to progess over the next 25 years, TPC courses will be the site of an estimated 75 percent of Tour events. Only the most historic courses, such as Pebble Beach, Riviera, and Colonial, will survive on the PGA Tour.

THE COURSE

TPC at Sawgrass set the standard for future TPC courses throughout the world. The most famous hole on Dye's target course is the 132-yard, par-3 17th. Golfers know 17 as the first island green. The tee sits behind the 16th green, and the green rests on an island in the middle of a pond. Golfers have to hit the target, or they'll never see their

A golfer who holes out on 18 with the same ball he teed up on the 1st tee has played a magnificent round because there are water hazards on all 18 holes. Putting is somewhat easier today than it was when Pate won the TPC. In response to numerous complaints about the greens, they were all redesigned with less undulating slopes. There are still slopes on the greens, but they are not as severe as they were in 1982.

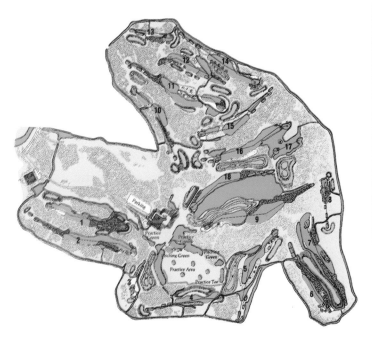

▲ The par-3 17th is among the most difficult par-3 holes in the world.

▼ The par-5 16th hole provides the last real birdie opportunity.

ball again. It's not uncommon to see players in The Players Championship splash down on 17 and double bogey as a result. Hitting the green is an accomplishment, but if the tee shot isn't near the pin a three-putt is likely. Avoiding the water on 17 doesn't necessarily mean you keep your ball much longer. The final hole is a 440-yard par 4 with a lake running down the entire left side, making it the toughest hole on the course. The hazard is close to the green, and it's easy to yank the ball into the place where Pate tossed Beman and Dye.

Although more people were playing golf in the 1890s, the overwhelming majority of them were wealthy. All the golf courses in the United States at that time were private clubs that restricted membership based on sex, religion, race, and financial status. This caused problems for people who didn't meet club restrictions but wanted to play the game. The only way they could get on a course was to find a club member who would invite them as a guest. Because clubs limited guests to one or two rounds a year, most nonmembers didn't even get a chance to play.

When Van Cortlandt Golf Course was built in 1895, that all changed. Some affluent residents of Riverdale, New York, a narrow Hudson River island slightly west of Bronx, were searching for land to start a private golf club when they discovered picturesque Van Cortlandt Park. Its hilly, wooded, lakeside landscape was the ideal setting for a golf course, so they petitioned the Bronx park commissioners to let them form their club on the public land. They were rejected because the city charter prohibited private and exclusive use of public land. However, the park commissioners were intrigued by the idea of laying out a golf course at Van Cortlandt Park and decided to build a 9-hole course for the public.

They located Tom Bendelow, who was a Scottish golf architect at A.G. Spalding & Bros., the first sporting goods company to sell golf clubs in the United States. Bendelow worked cheaply and fit into the commission's budget. Unfortunately, they got what they paid for. Bendelow went out to Van Cortlandt Park and marked the first tee with a stake. He hiked about a hundred yards and marked a bunker,

VAN CORTLANDT GOLF COURSE

•

Bronx, New York

•

6,122 yards, par 70

•

Designed by Tom Bendelow

•

Redesigned by
William Mitchell

A wooded hill separates the course from New York City buildings.

then another hundred where he built a mound, and a little less than a hundred to mark the green. All his greens were either round or square and had no sand traps.

Although Bendelow's design was primitive, he was the most active golf course architect in the late 19th century, making around $25 per design. His work was usually redesigned as golf's popularity grew. It was fortunate that Bendelow was available to design Van Cortlandt Golf Course because it allowed the commission to open a public course, leading more people than ever to take up golf in the New York area. Playing Van Cortlandt was much more affordable than joining a private club, and a golfer didn't have to deal with haughty restrictions. Van Cortlandt's success inspired other cities to open public golf courses. Today, 70.3 percent of all rounds of golf are played on public courses, thanks to the Bronx park commissioners of 1895 and Van Cortlandt Golf Course.

Because the New York Thruway was constructed through the original course, the modern 18th green is a mile away from the clubhouse.

THE COURSE

Like many historic golf courses, the current Van Cortlandt course is nothing like its original. As Bronx grew, the field and lake were integrated into the development of the community. Ultimately, the course was spread out over four different pieces of land around and away from the lake. For the most part, the modern Van Cortlandt is on the same land as in the 19th century, but the course had to be redesigned when the Major Deegan

Expressway was built between the clubhouse and the 18th green. When you tee up on the 210-yard, par-3 17th hole, you are standing where the old 18th green used to be. The 18th hole was moved about 350 yards away. It is now a 320-yard potential birdie hole that runs downhill. If the tee shot stays out of a fairway bunker, a birdie is likely.

Golfers playing the 620-yard, par-5 2nd hole are playing on land that was originally two short par 4s in Bendelow's design. As you walk up the elevated fairway, you see a flat mound where the old green was located. Then you see another flat mound where the old tee was. The modern green originally belonged on another hole.

Experiencing a round of golf on old public golf terrain is still enjoyable. There are no par 4s over 400 yards, but that doesn't mean all par 4s are automatic birdies or pars, especially the 389-yard 14th hole. It's a sharp dogleg right, and there is a large tree on the right side of the fairway. Even a well-hit tee shot that settles on the right side of the fairway will be blocked by the tree. Golfers have to be careful to place the tee shot on the left side in order to hit the green in regulation.

For the most part, the fairways are wide at Van Cortlandt. This is important because many of the golfers playing the public course are beginners or high handicappers. They need a generous golf course to allow them to play, which is precisely the reason the course was opened in 1895.

Above: *The 14th green sits next to a large lake, which is the center of both the park and the course.*
Below: *A small pond, the only water hazard in play on the course, complicates the par-4 13th.*

WORCESTER COUNTRY CLUB

•

Worcester, Massachusetts

•

6,422 yards, par 70

°

•

Designed by Donald Ross

As the level of outstanding golfers grew around the world, the Ryder Cup became even more interesting than when it began in 1927 at Worcester Country Club in central Massachusetts. The United States tended to dominate the Ryder Cup—that is, until the PGA European Tour blossomed. Once the Ryder Cup changed from the United States versus Great Britain and Ireland to the U.S. PGA Tour versus the PGA European Tour, there was no longer a dominating team.

The Ryder Cup was originally created to promote professional golf. The Walker Cup match was already successfully promoting amateur golf, but professional golf needed some help. A man named James Harnett, circulation manager of the original *Golf Illustrated* magazine, believed an international professional match would promote golf pros. He met with the PGA of America on December 15, 1920, to propose the idea of an international pro match. Initially, PGA President John Mackie was opposed to the idea. Because so many U.S. pros were from Scotland, he viewed the match as a free trip home for them. However, his dissent was overridden and the idea was approved.

The next year an informal match was held between U.S. and British pros and amateurs at Gleneagles Golf Club in Scotland. The British overwhelmed the Americans 9 to 3, mainly because most American pros didn't think the match was important and were concentrating on winning the British Open. U.S. player Jock Hutchison, a British native, won the British Open; the next year it was won by Walter Hagen.

Because the match was considered unimportant, it was not renewed until 1926. The Walker Cup was increasing in popularity. Samuel Ryder, a wealthy Englishman, wanted to help the professional matches adopt the same pattern—four-ball and single match play every two years back and forth across the Atlantic. Ryder donated a trophy from the Sheffield factory of Mappin and Webb.

A match was set at Wentworth Golf Club in Surrey, England, on June 4. The American team consisted of 10 players, only five of which were native-born Americans; the other five were foreign born. Once again, the British team demolished the American. They won 13 to 1 but were displeased with the victory because so many of the American players were from the United Kingdom. Because of this, the 1926 match was voided as an official Ryder Cup.

Willie MacFarlane conquered the immortal Bobby Jones in a 36-hole playoff in the 1925 U.S. Open.

Ted Ray, captain of the Great Britain–Ireland team, presented the Ryder Cup to the American victors in 1927.

When teeing off the hill on the 1st hole, a player must be careful to keep the drive short of the creek.

Both PGAs agreed to limit the members of the teams to players born in their own countries. Another match was staged the next year at Worcester Country Club; it was the first official Ryder Cup. Worcester Country Club was selected because it was the site of the 1925 U.S. Open in which Willie MacFarlane defeated Bobby Jones by one stroke in a 36-hole playoff.

Home course advantage was beneficial to the American team. Finally, they played well in an international match. Walter Hagen and Johnny Golden defeated Ted Ray and Fred Robson 2 and 1 in the first match. America won the next two best-ball matches and took a 3 to 1 lead at the end of the first day. Wild Bill Mehlhorn won the first singles match 1-up over Archie Compston. Johnny Farrell, Golden, and Leo Diegel dramatically won the next three matches. Gene Sarazen tied Charles Whitcombe, but Hagen and Al Watrous won the

next match. George Duncan's 1-up victory over Joe Turnesa was the only British singles victory, but it wasn't enough. The United States won the Ryder Cup 9 to 2.

The next Ryder Cup was held in England in 1929—the British won 6 to 4. The Ryder Cup was finally well-established after World War II. The United States dominated with 16 victories until 1983 when the PGA European Tour replaced Great Britain and Ireland as the PGA Tour's opponent. In 1987, Europe finally won again.

THE COURSE

I t's no surprise that Worcester Country Club was selected for the first Ryder Cup and the 1925 U.S. Open. As is common in a Donald Ross design, the greens make even good players look bad. Ross always

191

WORCESTER COUNTRY CLUB

believed in elevated, undulating greens. Two-putting a green at Worcester is an accomplishment, and one-putting is a miracle.

Demanding greens make Worcester difficult; combining them with five extremely difficult par 3s allows putts and tee shots to make or break a round. The first par 3 is the 232-yard 4th hole. It warns golfers to take the par 3s and greens seriously. The tee is elevated, but the hole doesn't play shorter because the green is also elevated. Most golfers miss the green. And, if they only pitch up 15 feet from the hole, they're likely to three-putt for double bogey because of a severe slope that can throw the approach putt six feet past the hole. The 179-yard 6th hole has an even higher green and is a bear to hit in regulation. The only par 3 that is reachable is the 177-yard 8th hole, which is rather flat. All it takes is a straight tee shot that avoids bunkers. The 161-yard 10th hole drops straight downhill to a tiny green contained by trees and bunkers. The par 3s end on the 196-yard 13th hole.

This doesn't mean the par 4s are easy. After surviving the 6th hole, golfers have to deal with a frightening tee shot on the 398-yard 7th. The tee sits on top of a hill behind a creek, and the fairway snakes to the right up a hill and around thick trees. It is easy enough to carry the creek but even easier to land in the trees. Even a good tee shot leaves a tough, uphill approach shot to a well-bunkered green. Finishing the front nine is an even more tedious task. The 410-yard, par-4 9th runs up a hill along a sloping fairway that is walled with trees waiting to steal tee shots.

The back nine isn't easy. The 420-yard, par-4 12th hole is similar to the 9th. Another long par 4 is the 462-yard 17th hole that starts on a tee looming 60 feet above the fairway. The hole goes downhill, and trees create a tight dogleg left on the last 160 yards of the hole.

The only real birdie opportunity comes on the 478-yard, par-5 5th hole. It has a water hazard in the middle of the fairway about 135 yards short of the green. The hazard can be carried in two shots, but the birdie putt is easy to miss. The shortest par 4 is the 326-yard 18th hole, but it is not a birdie hole. The fairway slopes up a steep hill, making the hole play at least 380 yards. Even worse, the green has deep bunkers in front that seize the blind approach from down the hill. Worcester Country Club is only 6,422 yards long, but, with so many tough par 3s, the total yardage is no indication of how the course really plays.

PHOTOGRAPHY

All photographs courtesy of the author except the following:

The publisher has made every effort to contact the photographers of all photographs appearing in this book.